Many
Roads
to Home

Many Roads to Home

New York to California

Virginia Wink Hilton

Copyright © 2021 by Virginia Wink Hilton

All rights reserved. No part of this publication may be reproduced, distributed, or transmitted in any form or by any means, including photocopying, recording, digital scanning, or other electronic or mechanical methods, without the prior written permission of the author, except in the case of brief quotations embodied in critical reviews and certain other noncommercial uses permitted by copyright law.

ISBN: 978-1-7368831-0-5
E-ISBN: 978-1-7368831-1-2
Library of Congress Control Number: 2021908919

Cover and interior design by Tabitha Lahr

Printed in the United States of America

Contents

Prologue 6
Culture Shock, 1956 8
SMU 12
Becoming Virginia Wink 25
The Edge of the Big Thicket 35
A New Life 37
Peavine Mountain, 1957 41
New Experiences 46
Becoming Parents 49
Hitchcock, 1962 59
Back to New York, 1967 76
A New Direction 79
The Inner Journey 84
Travel Adventures 94
California, Here We Come! 102
Expansion 112
California—Again! 115
Inner Journey II 122
Back to School 126
Family Time 130
The Kids 136
A Seismic Shift 154
My New Vocation 165
Fun—Finally! 171
The Man on the Beach 184
The Pearl of Great Price 194
California, Here I Come—for Good! . . . 204
The Wedding 215

Prologue

Summer, 1972
"Choose your medium—watercolors or chalk—and put on paper whatever emerges from your inner self," the wise woman instructed the group who had gathered at her retreat center in Napa Valley. "Don't think about it, just let it happen."

I stared at the paper, feeling nothing, listening to the New Age music in the background. Then, after a half hour or more there emerged on the paper a beautiful, brightly colored butterfly—with a large, open scissors, ready to clip its wings. I became still and sad. *That's it. That's now. But,* I thought, *all my life the scissors have never been far away.*

CULTURE SHOCK, 1956

It was 5 p.m.: The train arrived on time, the doors jolted open, and dozens of serious-faced people poured out ahead of us onto the dark platform. And suddenly they were gone. Walter and I looked at each other—we'd better get out of here before this door closes!

I leaned against the door to make sure it stayed open while we tugged at our luggage and boxes and pushed them onto the platform. We looked around us, and then again at each other. No conductor? No red caps? No. No one. We were absolutely alone.

We had arrived at Pennsylvania Station in New York City, our final destination. At the end of the platform we saw a wide staircase with so many steps we couldn't see the top. We hauled our stuff to the bottom of the staircase, but how were we going to get our belongings up those endless stairs? Walter picked up two suitcases and began trudging upward. I stayed behind with two more suitcases and two boxes, nervously looking around at the dark, cavernous surroundings and mumbling to myself, "My parents would have been happy to buy us airplane tickets!" But Walter had insisted we go by train from Houston to New York City—coach class—to save money. We had packed up our wedding presents in barrels and left them in Dallas, bringing with us clothing and minimal supplies to furnish our student rooms at Union Seminary, where Walter would begin his Bachelor of Divinity studies. I would go across the street to Barnard College for my senior year.

Leaving the suitcases on the edge of the landing, Walter raced back down the stairs where I was anxiously waiting. We then grabbed all that was left, and I pulled and tugged two heavy suitcases up one stair at a time, gasping for breath, resting in between. Finally, we reached the top with all our belongings safely intact, relieved, and not quite fully aware of all the risks that surrounded us.

"We made it!" Walter shouted with glee.

"I can't believe what we just did," I responded glumly.

We continued across the wide hallway of the terminal, making our way past small shops and food stands, slowly pulling, sometimes pushing a suitcase or kicking a box until, after what seemed an interminable amount of time, we managed to get through the revolving doors and out into the late afternoon light of New York City.

We looked around us, awestruck. The buildings, taller than any we had ever seen, the noise of traffic, the unique smells of the city—unbelievable! This was our new home. I clutched Walter's arm and tried to take it in. There we were, two fresh-faced, naïve kids from Texas, weary from travel, speechless, and excited by the first few minutes in this place that would change each of us forever.

"We'd better locate a taxi," Walter said, finding his voice. A gaunt man, leaning against his vehicle nearby, eyed us and our multiple carry-ons and sauntered over.

"Where to?" he asked, expressionless.

"Broadway and 122nd Street," Walter replied, his anxious voice clearly signaling that we had no idea where we were or where we were going. The man said nothing and began loading the bags and boxes into the trunk of his cab. We got into the back seat. How many cabs had we ridden in our lifetime? This might have been the first.

The taxi began its journey in a direction we thought might be north. We ambled through rush hour traffic, and after some time we began to see theatre marquees, with names of shows we would attend soon after. After the theatre district, the cab turned west and entered the West Side Highway, driving alongside the Hudson River until the George Washington Bridge was in sight, then back down through busy neighborhoods. Finally, the taxi pulled to a stop, and the street signs indicated we had arrived at our destination.

The cab driver turned to us and said, "That will be $34." Walter looked at me, panic-stricken. We didn't have that much money left! I sat frozen. What would we do? Then, with miraculous timing, out of the dormitory door emerged a familiar face. It was Walter's cousin, Dave, who was a third-year student! He recognized us and saw our distress. Walter shook hands with this relative whom he had seen only a couple of times, and had written to about our impending arrival at the seminary. Dave, a very quiet, studious sort of guy, paid the cab driver, giving him a stern look but saying nothing. As the cab drove away Dave informed us dryly that the fare should have been no more than $18—our first experience of being "taken" for a very long ride.

We entered the dormitory and dropped our belongings inside two small rooms on the first floor, where we would share the kitchen and bathrooms with other married couples. We were hungry and exhausted, and our cab ride had left us in a state of shock. But we were in for yet another.

In the evening, Dave took us to a little restaurant two blocks away on Morningside Drive. We ordered the cheapest thing on the menu—a hamburger for ninety cents. In our famished state we imagined the burgers would be like the ones we loved from the little stand near the SMU campus: juicy meat, curly lettuce, large tomato slices, pickles and onions on a bun dripping with mayonnaise, with tasty French fries—all for twenty-five cents! What arrived in front of us was a dry bun with a small, hard-as-rock meat patty. Period. The waitress plopped down bottles of catsup and mustard and walked away. We looked at each other in disbelief.

This is it? This is what we get in New York City? Help! We've died and gone to hell!

So how did we get from Texas to New York City? The story begins at Southern Methodist University in Dallas, Texas.

SMU

In the fall of 1953, I entered SMU, a different world for me. The girls in my dorm arrived in their cars from different towns across Texas and the nearby states of Oklahoma, Louisiana, and Alabama. They wore their stylish dresses, circular felt skirts, and saddle shoes. And many of them brought their mink stoles for winter.

Most were immediately engaged in sorority rush. Getting into the "right" fraternity or sorority was a priority for the majority of SMU students. Not me. Months before I had seen the movie, *Take Care of My Little Girl* (starring the popular actress, Jeanne Crain), which focused on the snobbishness of sororities, and the pain of exclusion. I found this "un-Christian," and I vowed not to join one. So, I attempted to find friends and a roommate among like-minded students. My mother, realizing immediately the significance of the Greek organizations on the SMU campus, said to me, "Why don't you go ahead and join a sorority, and then you can change their attitudes?" (She actually said that!)

"No, thank you," I replied. But, during the first semester, I slowly began to change *my* mind. The campus-wide focus on and commitment to these organizations rather quickly overcame my objections. At midterm, during the second round of sorority rush, I was a candidate. Pledging a sorority meant finding your social status. And that status was based upon a number of things: your family's financial level often played a big role, as well as popularity in high school and physical appearance. Judgments were made on both sides—by the sorority and the potential pledge. For me, the Pi Beta Phis were too rich, the Kappa Kappa Gammas were all blond (or so it seemed). The Kappa Alpha Thetas seemed just right. One of their leaders was a Methodist minister's daughter, and I thought that was a good sign. I chose Theta, and Theta chose me.

Betsy Singleton, a Dallas girl, Mina Fields, a like-minded freshman from Abilene, and Georgene Wollgast, from Denver, became my closest sorority friends. And friends we'd remain!

There was another organization that soon had my full loyalty: MSM, the Methodist Student Movement. Since SMU was a Methodist school, it drew other students who had a strong background in the denomination, and a commitment to its central characteristics: religious but not fundamentalist, a liberal perspective on social issues, and commitment to social action. A man named Bill was hired by MSM as leader and councilor of the organization, and he felt like a safe parent figure in the midst of the major life-change. And through MSM I made many friends, some of whom I would remain in contact with for life: Marty King (Brockway), Betty Crump (Hanson), Rebecca Sloan (Bowers), Helen Benton (Williams).

Sorority Sisters—40 years later

And then there were the boys. George Durson, Charles Scott, Pat Green. And Walter Wink. He was a year ahead of me, and he was a leader in MSM. We got acquainted through the meetings there, and we went out several times. But, to my disappointment, Walter began dating the beautiful Rebecca Sloan. That relationship ended when she switched her attention to a senior—the handsome football player and premed student, Malcolm Bowers, who eventually became her husband.

Through MSM a few of us formed a prayer group that met for a half-hour or so at lunchtime during the weekdays. Needless to say, we were "good" students—no smoking or drinking or "bad" behavior.

Because I believed my "calling" was to be a minister's wife, I was drawn to date pretheology students. Occasionally I accepted other dates. One night I went out with a member of SAE (known to be a partying fraternity). At the end of the evening, while parked in front of the dormitory, he attempted to kiss me. I demurred, since I didn't kiss on a first date. His closing comment to me was, "You're the kind of girl I want to marry, but not the kind I want to date." I was very pleased with myself!

For several months during my freshman year, I dated Pat Green. He was a cute, somewhat short, lively guy, and a "pretheologue." Pat, like Walter, was a member of Phi Gamma Delta fraternity, known as the "Fijis." Toward the end of spring, he invited me to their annual Fiji Island Ball. Dressed up in island attire—I in a sarong and he in a matching man-sarong, leis around our necks—we made our way to an extravagant outdoor luau. Before we joined the crowd, Pat took me behind a tree, pulled me close to him, and planted a big, open-mouth kiss on my lips. My reaction was one I'd never experienced before (even though I had certainly done a good bit of kissing by then). And I felt that powerful feeling through my entire body and down to my toes. But then I panicked. I thought to myself, *I'll never make it through college* [as a virgin]! As I was standing next to Pat in the darkness, suddenly an image of Walter ran through my head and I thought, *Walter will save me!*—meaning, he would save my virginity.

That's what I thought. That's what he projected. He was disciplined, scrupled, a committed Christian. I could count on him to do the right thing. To "save me."

The school year was almost over, and one evening after an MSM meeting, Walter told me that he was going to go to Oregon for the summer to work in a lumber mill. I mentioned to him that there was a CFO—Camp Farthest Out—meeting in Oregon and that maybe he should consider going. Camp Farthest Out was a religious retreat founded by Glenn Clark, a well-known author of spiritual books, and was held in different locations across the country. I had told him about my mother's initial life-changing experience at CFO, and my family's frequent attendance at the camps since. He was interested. He said we would keep in touch during the summer so he could get specific information.

We did stay in contact. And he went to CFO for a week, which turned out to be one of the most impactful of Walter's life.

When I returned to school after the summer break, I moved into Peyton Hall with my Theta friend, Betsy Singleton. We made good roommates, and she saw to it that things were kept neat and tidy. Betty Crump and Rebecca Sloan roomed across the hall from us.

Walter got in touch with me immediately, saying he wanted to tell me all about his experiences at Camp Farthest Out. We spent that first evening sitting in lawn chairs in his backyard. It was cool enough on that September evening, and the almost full moon added to the romantic energy in the air.

As we sat, inching the chairs closer and closer together as the night wore on, Walter described what had taken place during his week at CFO. He was inspired by the talks, the singing, the "devotions in motion" (soft exercises to music at the beginning of each day). The spiritual quality to the gathering was something quite new to him, and inspiring. One aspect was new to me; also attending this particular Camp was an unusual group of people who practiced *glossolalia*, "speaking in tongues." Walter was initially quite taken by this, and I was a little freaked out. But I listened intently and was thrilled that we now shared what had been quite significant in my life: Camp Farthest Out.

We looked up at the moon, held each other, and knew that a life together had begun.

I liked the courses I took my freshman year: social studies, Earth science, Spanish (as in the public schools of Texas, so poorly taught)—but it was my English course that confirmed my love of literature and locked me into my major for the next four years. In my junior year I was particularly fond of a philosophy teacher—an extremely smart, loveable old Texas guy (who pronounced Kant as can't). Another favorite was a course entitled the history of American ideas. (I have always regretted not learning more about European history, and not taking French.)

I got well acquainted with the professors in the English department, because during my sophomore year I became one of their secretaries. College was relatively inexpensive in those days. I think tuition was $300 a semester for me, as a Methodist minister's daughter. My parents had extra money at that time. But I felt that, with dormitory costs and sorority dues, I should help out. I worked for eighteen hours a week, enjoyed it, and developed secretarial skills that would prove useful a few years later.

I also continued piano lessons for the first two years, and practiced when I had the time and the opportunity. So, with this busy schedule—and other activities and a social life—my grade point average the first year was 3.5. After the relationship with Walter began, my study time actually increased a substantial amount. We never, or rarely, went to football games or movies, but went to the library for all our dates, even on weekends. My average increased to 4.0. Walter loved to study and had a compulsion to make the highest possible grades.

In the midst of focused studying, Walter and I continued to be quite active in the Methodist Student Movement.

We both were involved in various campus activities. There were occasional Fiji parties and dances, and I participated in Theta activities when they suited me.

Early in my sophomore year, the wife of Bill, the MSM leader, announced she would be directing a one-act play and would hold an audition for the roles. I don't recall the name of the play. But I do remember that central to it was the interaction between two prostitutes at the foot of the cross. I got very excited about auditioning, and Walter, who had had the role of Orsino in Shakespeare's *Twelfth Night* the spring before ("If music be the fruit of love, play on!"), went with me. I had not done much acting in high school, but I was drawn to the script, and apparently did a good job in the audition. The director offered me the role. I was so pleased and excited! On the drive back to the dorm with Walter, he was totally quiet and kept his eyes on the road ahead.

"What's the matter?" I asked.

He was silent for a moment, and then he replied, "I just don't like the idea of my girlfriend playing the role of a prostitute."

I didn't say anything. Inwardly, I was shocked. How could he feel that way? I so wanted to play this part. But I didn't want to upset my boyfriend. The next morning, I called up the director and told her that I would not be in the play.

Clip-clip. Snip-snip. My acting career was over before it began.

✷ ✷ ✷

I was standing beside Florence, Walter's mother, as we watched a fraternity touch football game behind my dormitory. I had been introduced to her a few weeks before as the new girlfriend. Florence often dropped by Walter's games, whether football or basketball, or anything else he did. This was the first time she and I were together without Walter. As she stared straight ahead at the players on the field, she said, "Yesterday I talked with my friend Mary, and she said she was very happy that her son's new girlfriend is very tall, just like he is."

I was stunned. My five-foot-two frame shook a little. In time that comment proved to be typical of Florence, in several ways. I would learn gradually that she didn't mean to be unkind or even critical. She just spoke her mind. She had very little sense of context or connection to what was going on. At a party or dinner table, she would sometimes blurt out a statistic or a factoid that was totally irrelevant to the conversation taking place. It would become clear to me years later that Florence would have been diagnosed with Asperger's.

Florence Wink was a very smart woman. She had attended Illinois University and was a Phi Beta Kappa her junior year. She was well read for the rest of her life (though very prudish about the type of novels she read or movies she saw). She was devoted to caring for her three children, whom she raised according to the Watsonian directives that were accepted by educated people of her generation: don't deviate from the schedule, don't spoil, don't praise, don't be affectionate, etc.

Florence's father had been the superintendent of a school. Her mother died when she was an infant, and her father remarried a large, somewhat inert woman who raised Florence and her sister—but she seemed to have had little or no emotional involvement with her stepdaughters.

While Florence was very attentive to her own children—the twins, Dick and Sylvia, and Walter who was eighteen months younger—she didn't have the capacity to be warm and fuzzy. Feelings and spontaneous affection seemed foreign to her.

Florence's husband, Ed, was a rather sweet, softer man. He was her intellectual inferior, and probably in many ways a disappointment to her. In their early years in Dallas, Ed was a partner in a business that produced oil field supplies. He had some sort of falling out with his partners and left the business. (The partners became leaders in the community, and their company became the multi-million-dollar corporation, Texas Instruments—a fact that was not lost on the family.) After his departure, Ed, who didn't seem to be cut out for business, took the family on a prolonged camping trip in New Mexico, which was one of the few memorable times the family spent together.

Florence's dream of moving to a beautiful home in Highland Park was never fulfilled. Ed eventually worked for his brother, who had a warehouse that sold paint supplies. Ed was the traveling salesman for the company, and Florence became the bookkeeper. Ed was away from home much of the time. On his trips he carried along a keyboard on which he composed a few simple, rather romantic songs, which he had some hope of publishing. That didn't happen. Florence, who was very knowledgeable of classical music, was quietly disdainful of his compositions.

The three Wink children responded to their upbringing in different ways. I don't know much about Dick's

Ed and Florence

childhood. When I met him, he was attending the University of Kansas in architectural engineering. He had a strong aesthetic and artistic interest, and appreciated fine clothes bought at Neiman Marcus. He suffered from severe allergies, and seemed to elicit a great deal of attention from his mother when he was at home.

Sylvia was a sweet, smart, and rather plain young woman. She liked outdoor activities and was quiet, good-natured, and easy to be around. Walter was the tall, unusually handsome Adonis in the family, outstanding at whatever he did. Besides always being a good student, he was active in sports, very involved in Boy Scouts, and a leader in campus activities.

Sylvia played the flute, and Walter played the piano. Florence made sure that they knew and understood a great deal about music. (I was astonished at Walter's knowledge of music, his recognition of a large classical repertoire and his understanding of structure and technique. However, I found his piano playing to be a bit stilted.)

While living in University Park, the neighborhood just north of SMU, the Wink kids attended Highland Park schools along with the elite families of Dallas. While Dick's experience must have fed his desire for status and wealth, Walter reacted with a distinct distaste for both. No doubt that reaction also steered him toward the social activism of his adult life.

The Wink family attended Highland Park Methodist Church. The minister was Marshall Steele, a graduate of Union Seminary. The Winks were devoted Methodists, respecting and adhering to Wesleyan doctrine and social gospel perspectives, taught through the gentle but sophisticated preaching of Dr. Steele.

* * *

It was the beginning of March 1956. I rushed out of my philosophy class and headed for the garden behind the SMU library where I was to meet my fiancé. Spring had come early, and I settled on a bench beneath a flowering dogwood tree, slowly breathing in the fragrance, attempting to calm my excitement.

Soon Walter appeared, tall and handsome, and sat down beside me. As we touched, energy surged in both our bodies, withheld by our determined commitment to premarital celibacy. Our wedding was three weeks away.

Walter began talking about his future, our future. In a few months we would move to New York City where he would begin graduate studies at Union Seminary, with the intent of getting a doctorate. He had a vision that he might become something close to a Billy Graham with a PhD. I was so proud of who he was—Phi Beta Kappa, Most

Outstanding Senior, a winner at everything he did—and who he surely would become. I looked up at him with adoring eyes. Marrying him was the fulfillment of all that my twenty years of life had prepared me for—and all that my parents would have wished for their daughter. Then Walter turned to me and said, emphatically, "Whatever it is that I can't do, I want you to fill in the cracks!"

"Oh, yes!" I replied, breathlessly. "Yes, I will!"

Years later, I would reflect on that scene in the library garden in Dallas, Texas. Living in New York City during the Aquarian sixties and seventies the world would change, my world would change. Like many women around me, I would begin to discover who I really was, what I needed and what I wanted for my life. An entire generation would leap into a new reality. Remembering Walter's directive, a slight smile would cross my face. "Fill in the cracks"? During those years one thing would become crystal clear to me: I was not made to be putty!

Becoming Virginia Wink

From the beginning of my sophomore year, Walter and I "went steady." And then after his summer away, I got "penned" (received the Phi Gamma Delta logo pen), and then we were engaged. Walter was trying to decide where to go to school next. He had been drawn to Yale Divinity, but I still had an undergraduate year to complete, and Yale wasn't open to women at that time. So Walter turned his attention to Union Theological Seminary, which was located near Columbia University in New York City. Barnard, a women's college, was across the street. The decision was made.

We also decided that, since Walter would be appointed to a church for the summer, it made sense to get married during our spring break. The date was set for March 24. Because of this disruption in my junior year, I gained permission to move out of the dorm after the first semester, and I went with my roommate, Betsy Singleton, to live with her and her parents in a nearby Dallas suburb until the marriage took place. It helped that I had inherited my grandfather's Plymouth following his death the year before.

Pinned!

Wedding photo

Walter and I happily began planning the wedding. The date preceded both our twenty-first birthdays, so we had to have our parents' permission to obtain the marriage license. The ceremony was to be held at my father's church in Beaumont, Texas, where my parents had moved from Bay City two years after my high school graduation. My mother and I went shopping for a wedding dress, the bridesmaids' dresses, and a "going away" suit for the honeymoon. I had my photograph taken in my wedding attire, and all was going well.

When spring break came around and Walter and I arrived at my parents' parsonage for the wedding, we were both shocked to see numerous card tables filled with presents: silver, china, pots and pans, sheets and towels. Two hundred and fifty gifts! Walter's response was: "This is terrible. We have to give this stuff to the poor!"

I was flabbergasted. *But*, I thought and didn't say, *these presents are from my father's parishioners—from Bay City and from Beaumont. The Beaumont people don't even know me. These gifts were given to us because they love my dad and mom.*

Family members arrived: Mom's family, the Moores, weren't far away, so they all came to Beaumont for the first wedding to take place among the eighteen grandchildren. There were fewer of my father's family, the Conerlys, who lived a greater distance away in Louisiana. And the Wink family came from Dallas. Our wedding party arrived from far and wide to participate and celebrate with us.

After the bridesmaids, the groomsmen, and Walter had taken their place in the church sanctuary, my robed father walked me down the aisle as the organist played

After the ceremony

Mendelssohn's "Wedding March". Then Dad moved to the pulpit and began the ceremony. As he spoke, I looked up at Walter. He was staring straight ahead.

And that was the way it continued. Throughout our vows Walter had a slightly shaky voice, and never looked at me. Not once. I was stunned.

We walked back up the aisle, man and wife. We met all the guests at the lovely reception following the ceremony, but in those days there was no drinking champagne or wine. And, sad to say, no dancing.

Afterward, I went back to the parsonage a block away, changed into my blue silk shantung suit and bandeau hat. According to custom we were showered with rice as we waved goodbye to our friends and loved ones.

Walter and I then drove down to Bolivar Peninsula, taking the ferry across to Galveston for the first night of our honeymoon. During the drive my new husband was silent, and again he didn't look at me. *What's the matter? What's wrong?* I went from stunned to devastated. I didn't say anything, but tears fell down my cheeks and onto my suit. On my wedding night. In retrospect, I am aware of how very young we were—not yet twenty-one! Walter was most likely overwhelmed by it all—and perhaps he was also frightened.

We arrived in front of the Galvestonian Hotel, exhausted and nervous. We found our way to our room. I was more silent than usual, still hurt and mystified by the absence of eye contact during the ceremony, and on the long ride to Galveston. My mother's sister, Ann, had sewn me a night-gown and robe for my wedding night—very proper and unexciting. But I suppose it was appropriate for this night.

Honeymoon in Acapulco

Because of the thoughts and feelings rambling inside our young, naïve minds and our weary bodies, it was not to be the most joyous—or sensuous—occasion.

My grandmother, Mam-ma, as I called her, had given us the money for a honeymoon in Mexico. The next day we drove to the Houston airport and flew to Mexico City.

After our first night there we went to the home of an American pastor and his wife who were missionaries in the city. (Walter had arranged this meeting, believing that doing so made the trip worthwhile.)

The following day we flew to Acapulco and stayed in a beautiful hotel on the beach. After a couple of days Walter began to feel ill. Suddenly red spots appeared on his body. We were taken to a local doctor who diagnosed him as having "three-day measles." We then had to stay in our room—no more swimming in the pool or basking in the sun on the beach! Not the happiest honeymoon. But we were married.

At the end of a long week we took the plane ride back to Dallas and we moved into a small garage apartment near the SMU campus. We returned to our studies, as Walter headed toward graduation and I completed my junior year.

* * *

It was a special day on the SMU Campus. After my philosophy class I walked across the campus toward the rotunda. Folding chairs had been placed in careful rows facing the steps. At the top was a lectern and a row of seats. A man in a uniform was adjusting a microphone, and several people with flash cameras were standing nearby. There was a certain excitement in the air as students and visitors were filling the seats.

One of the most highly regarded honorary organizations for women on the SMU campus was Mortar Board. Each year it elected a small group of women from the junior class who were considered most outstanding, based on grades and campus activities. And they were presented the "mortar board" at the "calling out" ceremony in late spring. I was excited to discover which of my friends would be honored.

As I walked up to join the growing crowd, I scanned the backs of the chairs, already mostly filled, to see if there was an empty one next to a friend. Suddenly, I stopped stock still. Two familiar figures were seated a few rows in front of me. No, it couldn't be! And yet it was. I was looking at the backs of my mother and my grandmother. And slowly the realization came over me. They were here because I was to be "called out," even though I wouldn't even be at SMU the following year! I raced over to the empty chair beside them.

"Mama! Mam-ma!" I squealed. "What are you doing here?" They hugged me, and Mother told me that she had been contacted by SMU about this very special occasion. So, of course they were here!

"We wondered where Walter was," she added. We looked around but didn't see him in the sprawling crowd. Then the ceremony began. And after a few names were called I heard my own. I walked quickly up the steep stairs, and the mortar board was placed on my head by the organization's president. What a thrill! I walked down amidst the enthusiastic applause, returning to my beloved family members. After a short time of chatting with those around us, my mother and grandmother, a bit tired from their journey, said they would go to their hotel and then meet us for dinner.

Where was my husband? I wandered through the crowd in search of him, but he wasn't to be found. After saying goodbye to my dear mother and grandmother, I hastily walked the short distance to our nearby garage apartment. I raced up the stairs, rushed through the door, and there was Walter, sitting at the small kitchen table with his book and notebook in his hands. Studying.

"Walter," I said, "I just got called out for Mortar Board! Didn't they tell you it was going to happen?'

He looked up from his book, and said, "Yeah, they told me."

"But why didn't you come?" I asked in disbelief.

Walter paused a moment, then looked back at his book and said, "I just don't think it's Christian to be doing stuff like that," he replied.

I was stunned. Shocked. *Not Christian?* For his wife of less than two months to be so honored? In addition to graduating *magna cum laude* he had been awarded Outstanding Senior just three months earlier in a campus-wide ceremony. Okay for him, but not for me? My problem was, I deeply felt the hurt, but not the anger. I didn't even recognize it.

But the wound was deep.

The Edge of the Big Thicket

Following Walter's graduation, and for the three months before we were to head to New York City, we managed to get assigned to a very small church north of Beaumont called Village Mills. The pastor and his wife had moved away—and left a filthy parsonage. I was shocked, because my family had always moved into perfectly clean homes, leaving ours spotless. But this one was dirty and smelly. It seemed its inhabitants hadn't scrubbed the refrigerator or stove or bathroom in months. We spent a week trying to make it livable.

The house was surrounded by forest and brush. That was because we were on the edge of what is called The Big Thicket, a large territory that was so dense, so "thick," that there were huge areas without roads or even trails. The small parsonage was a couple of feet off the ground, and under it was mud. At night wild pigs would come out of the forest, go under the barbed-wire fence at the edge of our backyard, and come under the house to oink and slop around in the mud. What a lovely summer!

I was very uncomfortable. One night before we left our garage apartment in Dallas, we watched the movie, *A Rebel Without a Cause*. Afterward, I had my first anxiety attack. I don't remember the details of the movie, but I know that the rebel within me was handcuffed. My rebel had no voice; her voice was silenced, her energy frozen. A rebel is angry, right? He or she rebels because needs aren't getting met, things are not right. Anger was not allowed, according to my beliefs. And how could the rebel appear, when I was living the life God had ordained?

One night in Village Mills I experienced another anxiety attack. I was really terrified. I said to Walter that I needed to go for a walk. I went outside by myself and headed down the gravel road in front of our house, hearing the sounds of owls and other wildlife coming from the thicket. I was praying for some kind of relief. I kept walking, coming onto the highway, looping back to the tiny church, and finally into the parsonage.

On that lonely walk I felt that something was terribly wrong with me. I didn't understand what it could be, why these feelings were showing up when I had what I wanted, what my parents and God wanted for me. I had no one to talk to about the hurts and disappointments of the wedding and before and after. I couldn't even identify them for myself. I had no one to talk to about the anxiety, no one to help me explore my inner Big Thicket.

I felt better when I got back to the house. But the anxiety—and depression—would appear again over the years ahead.

A New Life

Soon after our arrival in New York City, I awoke in the morning of the first day of my last year in college. I looked through my small closet for what I thought would be an attractive dress to wear for the occasion. I chose a multicolored, full-skirted dress I had bought for a reasonable price at Neiman Marcus before leaving Dallas. I said goodbye to my husband and walked the long block up Broadway to Barnard. As I got closer, I saw young girls jumping out of black limousines parked at curbside. They were wearing straight dark skirts and grey long-sleeved sweaters! I looked down at my dress with the sudden realization of the different world I was about to enter.

Barnard was indeed a different world from SMU, and a far better one in some ways. In that single year I received an amazing education. The English literature department had excellent professors, as well as outstanding visiting speakers. Early in the semester, we heard the lecture of a visiting Chaucer scholar from William and Mary. He was elderly and spoke with a strong Southern accent. After a few minutes, the classmate sitting next to me mumbled in her Brooklyn accent, "It's hard to believe that anybody with a Southern accent could be intelligent!" I cringed and looked away. (Interestingly, almost twenty years later, I was standing on the edge of the track field at Fieldston School, watching as my son, Chris, was breaking records. And there she was, that same woman, watching as her daughter raced for the same private school. I remembered her comment, and smiled to myself.)

I was required to take Spanish and pass the course with a B average in order to graduate in May. The professor, Señora Dacal, was from Madrid and spoke Castilian Spanish, which I found difficult to understand, let alone to speak. Once inside the classroom no English was spoken. The students answered questions and discussed the homework—which was reading *Don Quixote*—in Spanish. The class was many levels above any I had experienced in Texas.

Very important for me was a religion class taught by Mrs. Reinhold Niebuhr. (Her husband was the brilliant and amazing theologian, still at Union Seminary.) Ursula Niebuhr was highly intelligent and knowledgeable. She spoke with her upper-class British accent, wore the same grey wool suit almost all the time, and never applied makeup. I learned a lot from her, but there was one thing I had a problem with: The course was entitled "Religion in America," and in an observational statement, Mrs. Niebuhr lumped together Methodists and Baptists as evangelicals.

We are NOT the same as Baptists! I shouted inside myself.

At the end of the school year, after fortunately passing the tests with required grade levels, I was awarded

Graduation

the Bachelor of Arts diploma from Barnard College and Columbia University. My parents weren't able to attend, and Walter made one of the two ceremonies. I felt proud— and enormously relieved to receive my diploma.

Even during the busy first year in New York, with both of us in school, we took advantage of the cheap balcony seats ($5?) in theaters, and saw lots and lots of plays, on and off Broadway (*My Fair Lady, Westside Story, The Diary of Anne Frank, All My Sons*, to name a few). That was an education in and of itself. In addition, we loved going to museums: the Metropolitan, the Museum of Modern Art, the Natural History Museum, the Guggenheim, the Whitney. We also loved going to the Cloisters in upper Manhattan, enjoying the beauty inside and out. And, of course, Riverside Park was only a block away, which provided much outdoor pleasure on weekends.

We quickly became comfortable riding the subway and the buses. And I soon discovered Macy's and Gimbels down on 34th St. Once I went with a new Barnard friend, also the wife of a seminary student. I learned that her husband, Steve, was the son of the Swedish owner of Scandinavian Airlines, which had recently bought Macy's. We found the person who waited on us at Macy's to be quite impatient and rude. While we were trying on clothes in a fitting room, the employee came in and reprimanded us quite sharply for taking too much time. After the woman walked away, telling us to hurry up and get out, my friend, obviously feeling hurt and embarrassed, tucked her head and said quite softly, "She doesn't know that I own this place!"

Peavine Mountain, 1957

In the spring of our first year in New York, we began to think about how we would spend the summer. Walter got the idea of going out West and getting a job at a forest fire lookout station. He figured that few people would consider Nevada as a place to go for such a summer occupation, so he wrote to Reno and asked if there was a vacancy, mentioning that he wanted to be as far away from a city as possible. We were offered a job outside of Reno, on Peavine Mountain.

We had a great road trip to the West Coast, and I was delighted to discover that my husband was quite willing to venture off on side roads when they called to us. (My dear father, on our many summer trips, would never leave the main highway!) We especially enjoyed Sequoia National Park, and then Yosemite, where we crossed over the mountains into Nevada soon after the high road was cleared of snow and opened for summer travel. We finally arrived in Reno and headed for the Forestry Service office. The man in charge greeted us warmly.

"Hello, you two from New York City. Welcome to Nevada! You'll have a very interesting summer living on top of Peavine Mountain. Pull up a chair and I'll show you what you do on the job."

We did so, and listened attentively as he talked us through the routine that we would follow each day, all day long—and nighttime, too, as needed. We looked at each other, relieved that the work instructions seemed straightforward and easy enough. We said goodbye to our "boss" for the summer, stocked up on groceries, and headed out for Peavine Mountain.

After driving about five miles north of Reno, we could see the mountaintop ahead of us. At its peak it was 8,266 feet, 3,800 feet above the city. Peavine Mountain was completely bare. No trees, no green bushes, just brown scrub brush. We exited the highway and followed the winding dirt road up the mountain, finally coming to a series of switchbacks. The last one bumped us up to the peak. We brought our car to a stop in front of a wooden building, fourteen by fourteen feet with wide glass windows all around. At each of its corners, cables were attached that were bolted into the ground, sending the relieving message that our summer home would not be blown off the mountain top!

We left our car in silence, walked the few feet to the summit, and stepped inside the lookout station. There was a double bed, a small table, a couple of chairs, a sink, two hot plates, and in one corner the radio equipment into which we would be reporting all day (and, when needed, in the night). The shower and toilet were outside. Clothes stayed in our suitcases under the bed. Not exactly a four-star resort for the next three months!

Virginia Wink Hilton | 43

Peavine Mountain

Immediately we began to study the maps to get acquainted with the territory as far as we could see. We learned how to operate the radio system, how to use the proper reporting lingo, how to recognize "legal" fires. And then we went to work, which meant keeping a sharp lookout in all directions, all the time. Over the summer we reported lots of smoke, but rarely were there dangerous fires.

Peavine Mountain didn't draw tourists in those days. The rare folks we saw were stragglers, sometimes gold diggers, and occasionally bivouacking servicemen from nearby Stead Air Force Base. Once a week one of us went down the mountain and into Reno for groceries and other supplies. That was a difficult time for me. I couldn't decide which was scarier: the terrifying drive down and back on the one-way dirt road, or staying alone in the station for a good part of the day. There were only a couple of times that some wanderer came into view, a little closer than was comfortable.

One morning after Walter had left for town on grocery duty, I began to change from my pajamas to clothes for the day, when suddenly a jeep full of servicemen bounded into sight at the end of the switchback. I was in full view, and there was nothing to do but fall on the floor. I stayed there until I could hear the jeep driving away. The soldiers were probably having quite a chuckle on their way back down the mountain.

Halfway through our Peavine stay, we had a family visit. My parents and my two brothers, Warren and Bill, drove all the way out from Beaumont, Texas, to spend a few days with us. And yes, we all stayed in the lookout station! Mom and Dad had the bed, of course, and we and the boys were on the floor on sleeping bags. Later, the Forestry

Service sent a staff member up to be on duty while we took a two-day vacation. We drove down to Lake Tahoe for the great, much-needed break, where my brothers waterskied and Walter and I discovered a lookout station above the lake, manned by another couple on college break. (*Oh, dear,* I thought—miffed, but silent, of course—*we could be here overlooking the beautiful water, with trees and blossoms all around, if it hadn't been for that letter saying we wanted to be far from civilization!*)

It was great for both of us to have those days with my family. The only good thing about saying goodbye was that we got our bed back. The rest of the summer it was just us. All the time. On the lookout for fires.

Then one night, not long before we packed up to go back to the East Coast, a very strange, disturbing, and unbelievable thing happened. We had gone to sleep at the usual time on a dark night. Suddenly we were both jolted awake by the brightest light all around us. And then in seconds it was pitch dark again. We looked at each other, mystified. What happened? How could this be? It was a while before we heard on our radio that an atomic bomb had been detonated on the Nevada site about four hundred miles south of us!

Needless to say, we wondered and worried about possible radioactive fallout. Did being at our elevation put us in danger? A lot of questions and fears. Of course, our experience didn't compare to being in or closer to a target zone. Yet, I feel it surely strengthened the beliefs we shared toward nonviolence and activism, and contributed to Walter's living them out in very significant ways in later years.

At the end of August we packed our belongings and loaded up our car for the trip back to New York.

New Experiences

After our return from the summer in Nevada, I was grateful to be offered a job. I was hired by a woman who was an editor for Scribner's Publishing. I was to be the line editor for a book which explored the theory of the "just war." I wasn't crazy about the book and its subject, but I did enjoy the editing process during that relatively brief period of time. I learned a lot, which served me well over the following years.

While I was growing up, I never excelled in or participated much in any kind of sports. (A summer on the swim team was the exception.) Ballet classes and tutus were unheard of in the small Texas towns where we lived. But a wonderful thing had happened at SMU. I took a modern dance class for physical ed. credit—and I loved it! It felt so right for my body and my mind. I would learn many years later that my "mixed dominance" (ambidextrousness) made it quite difficult to shift from right to left and back again (as in line-dancing). But modern dance was free flowing and creative. I had found the expression of the body that was right for me.

After graduation I was able to take some classes at the Hanya Holm Studio, and soon got together with a group of students and wives at the seminary who were also interested in creative dance. We easily found excellent dancers from local companies to provide weekly instruction.

In our third year at the seminary, I got the idea of creating a musical talent show. While there was a highly respected speech and drama department at Union (headed by Robert Seaver, who later became my boss) which produced plays each year, this more casual idea of giving students the chance to do their thing was widely appealing. I pulled together a committee and set about involving students from the music school. They wrote scores, others designed sets, and the newly formed dance group choreographed the final number. The show title was *Manhattan Moods*—each act set in various parts of the city. The climax took place in the "drawing room" of the president of the seminary, Henry Pitney Van Dusen and his very Downton Abbey British wife, joined by the John Knoxes and other faculty couples, who sang songs from Gilbert and Sullivan. Members of our dance group closed the show. It was a huge success. (Professor Seaver sat in the back, looking a little envious.)

Another new experience was extremely significant for me. Since the days just after our wedding, I had experienced periodic bouts of major depression. I was very fortunate to have been directed to a therapist who had just returned from Switzerland, where he had studied at the Carl Jung Institute. His name was Henry Elkin. I immediately felt safe and seen in sessions with him. He focused on dreams from a Jungian perspective, but also maintained a Freudian viewpoint.

After a time, Elkin suggested that, in addition to my individual sessions, I join his therapy group. What an experience that was! It was a varied group of several Jewish men, including one member who became a well-known psychoanalyst and writer. There was only one other woman, with whom I quickly bonded. I soon realized that this was my first ongoing and intimate exposure to a nonparochial group of people outside a religious setting. It opened my perspective considerably, and I found it quite a relief. While the periods of depression continued, I gained much emotional help and stability from both the individual and group therapy, as well as a broadening understanding of my own life experience and personal needs. I'm deeply grateful for that experience with Henry Elkin and all the group members.

Becoming Parents

May 1, 1958, was an amazing day for us. A few weeks after our return from Peavine Mountain, I discovered I was pregnant. The pregnancy was difficult from the beginning. I had morning sickness throughout the (almost) nine months. But I kept busy. About a month before the due date, I began to have symptoms and my obstetrician, Dr. Laird, a truly kind and attentive person, had me enter Presbyterian Hospital. I was to be with the baby in the rooming-in unit—where infants stayed beside their mothers. But first I was in a hospital room under observation for several days. Then, in the middle of the night on May 1, I began to have contractions. The doctor was called, and so was my husband.

Dr. Laird had me wheeled into the operating room. The baby was coming out feet first, and she reached in with a tool to assist his emergence. Particularly because he was premature, she did not use any medication or anesthesia. In a short time, I had a baby boy in my arms—four pounds, thirteen ounces! Walter and I were given some time to welcome our son, Stephen Philip—and we had never been happier! I experienced a "high" like never before. Rapturous! They took the baby away and placed him in an incubator for warmth for twenty-four hours. Then he was brought to me in the rooming-in unit, and he lay by my side for the rest of the standard two-week stay. I nursed him, talked to him, and felt such pride and joy. After a week the pediatrician showed up, and I saw her astonished look when she checked his chart. He had already gained weight! By the time we left the hospital he weighed well over five pounds.

What a blessing! What a joy!! For my mother (who became Noni) and my grandmother, too.

Stephen Philip with Noni and Mam-ma

After Walter completed the third year at Union Seminary, we spent the summer in Texas, and then we returned to begin his three years in the doctoral program. We no longer had seminary lodging and were expecting to move into Grant Houses a few blocks away. When we arrived in New York City, our apartment was not yet available. Our friends, Jim and Dottie, invited us to share their apartment while we waited.

One afternoon Dottie and I were in the apartment with our two toddlers, hers and mine, preparing dinner. In the kitchen area in front of the sink was a cart on which she had an electric pot with water boiling for pasta. The cord for the pot was plugged into the only AC plug in the apartment, under the kitchen sink. Little Stevie was toddling around the area, and I was close by. Suddenly something on the cart grabbed his attention, and he went quickly toward it. He stumbled and fell forward, his arm falling against the cord, which pulled the pot over, spilling the boiling water on top of him. And I was only a few feet away. I screamed and Dotty came in. She picked up Steve and we ran into the bathroom, turned on the water and splashed it all over him. I called our pediatrician and she told me to go right to the ER at St. Luke's hospital. I carried my crying baby down the elevator and out to the street and got into a cab.

At the hospital the head ER doctor determined that my son had burns over 90 percent of his body. He was quieted with a shot and then bandaged, with only his face and his hands showing. But after a short while the doctor ordered that the bandaging be removed so that they could take photos, and then they bandaged him again. I stood by, horrified.

I kept wondering, where is my husband? Was he shot on the street? Finally, around nine thirty p.m., after about a four-hour disappearance, Walter came into the ER. He had gone to another emergency room—at Columbia Presbyterian—to get treated for an infected toenail. He was delayed over and over by people who came in with more serious emergencies, such as gun wounds. And he didn't have any way to telephone.

Around ten p.m. the staff told us that they had done what they could, and—as was generally the case in those days—that parents were not allowed to stay overnight. How could that be? We were devastated! So we went back to our friends' apartment and left our baby in the hospital—alone. The next morning when we returned to St. Luke's, we saw the completely bandaged little Steve, lying in his hospital bed, his head and hands swollen several times their size, and completely black!

After a week of trudging back and forth to St. Luke's to spend daytime hours with our son, Walter and I made an appointment with Dr. Loomis, who headed the Psychiatry and Religion Department at the seminary. We recounted the traumatic event, the two-week hospitalization, alone at night, how on the second or third day the doctors thought Steve might have contracted spinal meningitis, and the constant injections of antibiotics as a result. Dr. Loomis was sober in informing us about the impact of this entire traumatic experience. He said, "As a result of this your son is likely to be schizophrenic." Walter and I both looked at him with shock, and we didn't speak. But after a few moments I felt an unfamiliar voice deep inside me scream, *No, he won't!* Years later, as I recalled that meeting, I seriously doubted that Dr.

Loomis had actually made such a prognosis. Perhaps, as he indicated the seriousness and the impact of all the factors, Walter and I jumped to the conclusion of schizophrenia. But that's what we both thought we had heard. And the determination was so strong in me: *That's not going to happen!*

Sometime later, Steve would tell us that he had a memory of being in his hospital room:

"I came out of my body and I floated up to the ceiling," he said. "Then I looked down and saw my parents. Mommy was crying, and Daddy was praying. That caused me to go back down into my body."

Overwhelming alarm . . . and intense gratitude!

After two weeks of unbelievable stress and anxiety, we brought our son home from the hospital. He couldn't walk at first, but the good news was, his eyes were bright, and he smiled. *Heaven*! We paid close attention to him during the growing up years.

Steve with his Mommy and Daddy

A couple of blocks down Broadway from the seminary was the entrance to Morningside Gardens, a complex of apartments, many of which were occupied by people connected to Union and Columbia University. Across the street were Grant Houses, apartment buildings referred to as "the projects"—low-income housing established by the city. Several apartments had been made available for Union and Columbia students for minimal rent. We felt very fortunate to be able to move into this two-bedroom apartment on a high floor in one of the buildings.

There were only three other white families living in the building—two from Union and one from Columbia graduate school. The rest of the residents were Latino and Black. We didn't interact much, but in general, we felt safe there. Several times we heard the sounds of fights and their aftermath (police sirens). But mostly we were comfortable. And we were so grateful that the low rent allowed us to complete graduate school debt free.

While Walter was in class each day, I pushed Steve in the stroller up the hill to the seminary, where he was in daycare, and I worked as a secretary in Bob Seaver's office. On weekends we continued to explore the city with our little toddler in tow.

From very early in his life Steve became attached to a lovely soft, silky blanket that had been a shower gift before his birth. He slept with it, and we carried it with us in the stroller when we went for walks or to the playgrounds. One day, when we came home from an outing, we realized with horror that we didn't have the blanket! It must have fallen out of the stroller when we were preoccupied and didn't notice. Very soon Stevie began to cry for his "blankie." There was nothing we could do. He didn't sleep, and the crying was continuous. We tried to distract him, offered other blankets and other treats, but he was inconsolable. The next day I went downtown to try to find a replacement. Nothing I saw looked like his lost love. The fabric was not nylon but more a silk or satin. After combing through dozens and dozens of baby blankets and coverlets in Macy's and Gimbels and other stores, I finally saw one that was made of a similar fabric. The only problem—it was white, and Stevie's blanket was a golden beige.

"Oh, well," I said, desperately. "I'll take it." When I explained the dilemma to the salesperson, she advised me to soak it in tea to change the color.

"Okay," I said. "I'll try anything."

When I got home, I found my son had been crying nonstop while I was away. I hurried to the kitchen and soaked the new blanket in tea for a few minutes. I hung it up to dry over the shower curtain in the bathroom. I realized it hadn't changed color much, so I would make a sink full of tea and try again. A few minutes later Walter carried the crying Steve into the bathroom to get a medication. As he walked past the bathtub Steve saw the blanket hanging on the curtain rod. He reached up, grabbed it, pulled it to him, and instantly fell asleep! His Mom and Dad felt enormous relief! (We had the blanket cut in two, just in case.)

* * *

On the evening of January 23, 1961, I was nine months pregnant. While washing dishes after dinner, suddenly there was a gushing waterfall from my body to the floor.

"Oh!" I cried. "Time to get ready!" Very early the next morning, experiencing mild contractions, I called my doctor, and she instructed us to get to the hospital immediately.

Around five thirty a.m., Walter and I went outside into the snowy street and hailed a cab, which drove us north to Presbyterian Hospital. All went smoothly and easily through the next hours. Dr. Laird ordered very little ether at the height of the pain, so I was fully conscious throughout the entire process.

"It's a boy!" the doctor announced enthusiastically. The baby and I were taken back to the rooming-in unit, where we were settled into our sleeping places. Walter and I soon gave the name of Christopher Warren to our new family member. After sleeping for a while, I awoke and looked over at my little son. He was sleeping soundly and calmly. He seemed to be at ease and at peace. There was a very special energy emanating from his body. I thought to myself, *This boy is going to grow up to be President someday.* (Well, I'm glad that didn't happen.)

My attention was drawn to the woman in the bed next to me who had also just given birth to a son. Her husband came into the room and they took turns holding their baby, who they named Steven. As the days wore on, we chatted between times of feeding and sleeping. I learned that her name was Linda Grover, and her husband, Stanley, was an actor and singer who had appeared in some of Broadway's most famous musicals. (They had a daughter, Cindy, born very near the same time of our Stephen's birth, and a few

Christopher Warren

Steve and his baby brother

years later a son, Jamie, who was the same age as our daughter. Despite many changes over the years, including the deaths of both Grover parents, the connection that was established with the three children would continue.)

After the standard two-week stay, we happily brought our second son home to meet his big brother, and to become a part of the city life we so enjoyed.

Hitchcock, 1962

Six years. Six years since that bleak arrival in New York City, and the feeling of, *What are we doing in this strange place? How can we survive here?* But during those six years I had become a New Yorker.

And now we were leaving. As the family entered the Lincoln tunnel, going into the dark unknown, there was a heaviness, like grief.

After his seminary studies, Walter had completed the three-year course for his doctorate. All that was left was his dissertation. Now what? In the early years at Union, Walter had considered going to Africa as a missionary after graduation. But in 1962, John F. Kennedy was President and Martin Luther King Jr. was igniting the civil rights movement in the South. Walter and I wanted to be a part of it. So, we decided to return to Texas where Walter would be appointed to a congregation by the Texas Conference of the Methodist Church.

The Ford station wagon was packed to capacity, and the boys—Steve, five years old, and Chris, a year and a half—occupied the smallest space possible. We were each leaving behind so many unexpected experiences and friends, a world that had expanded our universe many times over.

Walter glanced over at me. "You're sad to leave."

"Yes.," I replied. "This is really, really hard."

What I didn't say out loud was, *I don't want to do this! I want to support civil rights, but I don't want to go back to Texas.* Since I was twelve or thirteen, I had believed I was meant to be a minister's wife. I had imagined that role to be the most fulfilling possible. But now, how different I felt! I feared the life beyond the end of the tunnel to be bleak, lonely, and stifling.

The trip was long and uneventful... except in St. Louis, where we stayed overnight with my college friend, Georgene, whose husband was in medical school. When we awoke in the morning, we discovered that our car had been broken into and all our belongings stolen—including notes and pages from Walter's dissertation. (At that time there was no such thing as "saved on a computer"!) We felt overwhelmingly frustrated and helpless.

"We really *are* beginning from scratch!" Walter remarked, as we continued the journey.

Fortunately, and astonishingly, Walter's parents had insurance that covered the theft, so we were able to buy a simple wardrobe in time to attend the Texas Conference of the Methodist Church. For the service of induction into the fold, Walter had a new dark blue suit, and I wore a yellow organdy dress and a Jackie Kennedy-style hat that was covered with daisies.

For the impressive ceremony, the vows (if that is indeed what they were called) were read to Walter by a middle-aged man who was the only other person in the Conference at that time with a doctorate. (And thus the church leaders tipped their hat to Walter and his education.)

The Methodist Church is organized so that each year the Bishop and his cabinet of District Superintendents appoint or reappoint ministers to their congregations. At the end of the week-long annual conference, on Friday, the appointments were read, and the following Thursday everybody moved. (Method-ists indeed!)

The Bishop appointed Walter to Hitchcock, a coastal town of 5,280 people across the causeway from Galveston. He would be the pastor of a church of sixty members (with one college graduate). Most of the men in the congregation worked in the oil refinery in nearby Texas City.

On Thursday our family moved into the furnished parsonage next to the small A-frame, white brick church. And there we began a life that was as far as could be imagined from the one we had just left behind.

Walter plunged into his duties—weekly sermons, meetings, visits to parishioners. Soon it seemed he was gone most of the time, and when he was at home he worked hard on his dissertation. I tended to the boys, got to know the women, joined the church choir, and became a substitute pianist and organist.

Soon after arriving in Hitchcock, I visited the little in-home "beauty parlor" of a church member who was a hairdresser. While I was under the dryer the woman, Charlene, began to smoke a cigarette. "I'll have one," I said, somewhat sheepishly.

I had never smoked—until that moment. I puffed and blew while Charlene sat quietly, looking a little uncomfortable and avoiding eye contact. *The minister's wife, smoking?*

After a few coughs, I put out the cigarette—for good. Physically it was a miserable experience. Yet my little act of defiance gave me a sense of relief. I naively assumed that this was a privately shared moment between Charlene and me. But no doubt the hairdresser was on the phone as soon as I left her house. "Do you *know* what just happened?"

Behind our house there was a large empty lot completely filled with wild brush. The boys soon enjoyed wandering through the "weeds," as they called it. They also had lots of space for running and playing between our home and the church. Across the street was the grammar school.

During the summer we bought our boys a Slip 'N Slide. The boys jumped on one end of the skinny piece of plastic with the hose attached and joyously slipped and slid all the way to the other. They were surprised and delighted at how much fun it was. This activity kept up for several hours before we could get them back indoors. Unfortunately, there was a problem: As parents (who had lived in New York City for the past six years) we had forgotten about the impact of being outdoors on a hot summer day on the Gulf Coast without sunblock! By nightfall both boys were feeling miserable, looking red and swollen. The next day they couldn't get out of bed. We did our best to make them comfortable, applied ice packs and aloe vera, and hoped for the best. But it took the rest of that week for the two little boys to get back to normal. After that, we were committed to doing a better job of applying sunblock at the beginning of each sunny day!

By the end of that summer we found that there was a woman, Miss Emry, who taught kindergarten in her home in Hitchcock. On the first day we left Steve at her house and several hours later came back to bring him home. Miss Emry rushed up to me, waving a sheet of paper. "Look, look what he did!" she almost screamed, obviously quite disturbed. She showed me the paper, which had a drawing of a rabbit in its center that was completely obscured by lines drawn with a black crayon all across the page.

"He didn't stay in the lines!" she shrieked. "And he used a *black* crayon!"

I showed the drawing to Walter when we arrived home. "Hmm," he said. He then turned to Steve and said, "Tell us about your drawing."

"It's a rabbit at night!" he replied, with a twinkly smile on his face.

We did not take Steve back to Miss Emry's kindergarten class.

The closest preschool was in Galveston at an Episcopal church. So, for that first year I drove across the causeway to Galveston Island every school day, to give Steve a very sufficient kindergarten experience. "Crifferter," as Stevie called his little brother, was with me most of the time. We found ways to fill the hours while we waited for school to be over. We went to a library and I read him stories. Or we explored the town, and even went to the harbor and observed the big ships that were docked there.

Our explorations were the beginning of my plan to visit, whenever possible, places where things were made. I took the boys to a Coca-Cola bottling company, a bakery where bread and rolls were made, and eventually to a salt mine, to name a few.

One afternoon we were riding back into Hitchcock after a day in Galveston. Steve, who was looking out the window from his back seat in the car, suddenly cried out in

Steve and Chris

astonishment: "Mommy, Daddy—I just saw a Nee-gro!" *Like he's never seen a Black man before?* I thought. And he lived in the projects for three years! Well . . . he's in Texas now.

One day while I was cooking in the kitchen, Chris came bursting in, frightened, but not crying.

"Mommie," he said. "Janie shot me in the eye!" I quickly found out that the nine-year-old girl who lived two blocks away from us had shot him with her BB gun! The bullet was lodged right next to his eyeball. (Yes, even very young kids in Texas had BB guns.)

I rushed Chris to the one doctor in town. He got out his tweezers and extracted the tiny bullet in a second.

"Son, are you lucky!" the doctor said. "If that bullet had gone any further to the left—any further at *all*—you would've lost an eye!"

Needless to say, we were enormously relieved and grateful for the near-miss—then and forever after.

※ ※ ※

A great advantage to living back on the Gulf Coast was proximity to my parents—Noni and PaPaw, as their grandkids called them.

After I went to college, my parents bought a beach house on Bolivar Peninsula. High on stilts, the house was at the back of two oceanfront lots—but not far enough from the water to survive Hurricane Carla in 1961. Everything was washed away. My dad found a fifty-cent piece in the sand. That was it.

A few years later, they bought another house on the peninsula closer to Galveston in Crystal Beach. This time, while they were on the beach side of the highway, the house

Crab fishing

was far enough back from the waterfront to feel secure when another hurricane came through. This was the site of many wonderful family gatherings. And each summer, my kids would spend several weeks there with their beloved grandparents. Along with all the swimming activities and playing in the sand, the boys (and later our daughter) would go fishing with PaPaw. Sometimes for crabs.

One of the ultimate delights of the Gulf was the seafood, particularly the crabs. Dad would get chicken necks from a little store on the intercoastal canal. Then he and the kids would drop the chicken necks into the water and pull up the lines, which almost instantly would have several crabs clinging desperately to the unfamiliar meat. Back in the beach house, the crabs would be boiled. Then everyone was given a cracker to get through the shells and pull out the fresh, delectable meat. Sometimes it went into gumbo with okra and tomatoes, but mostly just got gobbled up with great spicy cocktail sauce. The best crabmeat ever!

Another inevitable treat at the beach was Dad's barbecued shrimp. Since he was a fisherman by hobby, the only seafood I ever knew him to buy was shrimp, which he always got right off the boat that brought them to shore. He then put them into a pot, shells on, with lots and lots of fresh bay leaves, chile powder, and tomato paste, and cooked them until done. They were then brought to the table—along with lots of napkins—and the scrumptious, hands-on feast began!

✳ ✳ ✳

While I enjoyed interacting with the Hitchcock church members, I felt a hole in my life. The artist in me was needing an outlet. I was fortunate to meet the Presbyterian preacher's wife and two other women, not in our church, who wanted to form a group where we could focus on art. Pomona liked to draw and paint (and later she became very well known for her work), and Sheila, too, was an active artist. Mary and I were the preacher's wives who were busy but knew the importance of staying connected to art and literature. We read art books and novels and talked about our everyday concerns. Then, suddenly, Betty Friedan landed among us: *The Feminine Mystique*. Wow! As we read and discussed the book it was like some unknown elixir was slowly transfused into our veins. Strange and exciting and scary, it opened up longing and emboldened discontent.

The other women in the little group loved to draw or paint or craft. Not I. I wanted to dance. But, how could I? Walter discovered that a high school friend of his was living in Galveston with her husband, a medical student. After we got acquainted, she and I organized a group of medical students' wives for a weekly creative dance class—which I taught. It was absolutely a lifesaver for me! We developed a program that the group performed in our church and in several others. A writer at the *Houston Chronicle* heard about us and came out to take photos. A several-page article with many photos appeared in the magazine section of the Sunday *Chronicle*:

July 4, 1965

Creative dancers worship God through the
LANGUAGE OF MOTION

"The Galveston group meets weekly for an hour devoted to study of modern dance technique, and

a half hour to creative activities. . . . Each dancer does her own improvisations on the choreography of a poem, a psalm, an idea. . . . Interpretation in movement has been given to T. S. Eliot's 'J. Alfred Prufrock,' Dylan Thomas' 'The Hand That Rules the City,' e.e. cummings' 'when faces called flowers...' Also, the group has interpreted Psalms 8, 100, and 23, given characterizations from the Prologue to the Canterbury Tales and devised a jazz routine to the popular record, 'Washington Square.'"

The author/photographer quotes me throughout the article, and ends with my words:

"The least that can be said for creative dance is that it provides a creative and meaningful outlet for physical and emotional energies, an activity of self-expression which can help to free a person from the superficial inhibitions which limit his relations with others and his services to God in the world."

In the weekly classes there was the opportunity to dance out unspoken feelings, and also to give form and shape to what was personally meaningful. The occasional performance in a church service was particularly enjoyed by the participants. After five years of being in hot water most of the time for involvements in civil rights and other issues, it was my dance group's performance during the Palm Sunday service which brought the wrath of the church hierarchy down upon my husband's head. It was that flap which led Walter to ponder whether to change directions for the future.

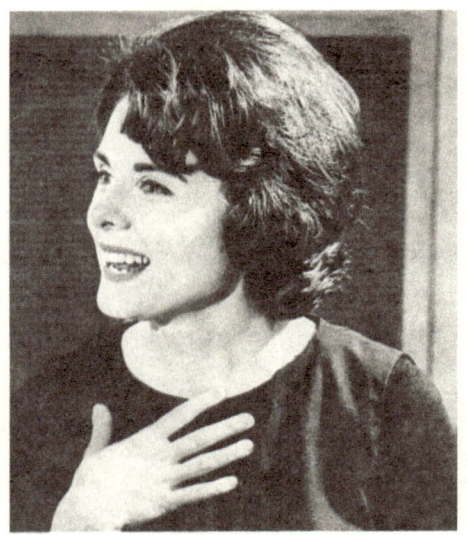

In the Houston Chronicle

The Creative Dance Group

A big change soon occurred in our family. I loved my little boys *so* much, and we had considered that two children might be our limit. Yet, when I was shopping in a store and passed by the girls' clothing section, I found myself looking longingly at a little dress or a bonnet, and feeling sad that I didn't have a daughter. Then one day I was thrilled to find that I was pregnant. *Maybe it will be a girl*, I thought, but didn't say out loud.

Morning sickness began at the beginning, as it had in the previous pregnancies, and stayed with me for the entire nine months. (I found with each pregnancy there was one particular edible that eased the nausea considerably: with Steve it had been Wheat Chex, with Chris it was a fudgsicle, with Becca it was peanut butter! Interesting, the things we remember!)

I found an obstetrician in Galveston who seemed responsive, but I knew he would be very different from Dr. Laird. (She had avoided anesthesia: none with Steve, a few whiffs of ether for Chris.) And, to my great disappointment, there was no rooming-in unit to be had.

Steve was several weeks early, Chris right on time, and Becca was late. She weighed more than the boys did. When I began to have contractions, Walter rushed us over the causeway to the hospital in Galveston. I was placed in a two-person room and told that the other occupant was delivering her baby. After a time, while my contractions were getting stronger, the roommate was wheeled in. Several of her relatives followed. And then her doctor and two other staff people walked through the door and stood at the end of her bed.

"We are so sorry to tell you . . ." Her baby had died. I instantly felt sorrow and panic. I was relieved when my doctor appeared and had me wheeled into the operating room.

The contractions were getting very strong. Dr. Richmond ordered the anesthesiologist to give me a spinal, assuring me that it would ease the discomfort considerably. But it didn't. As the baby pushed, my legs began to feel numb, and the pain grew more and more intense, almost unbearable. What happened? By the time the baby was emerging, it had become clear that the anesthesiologist had made a mistake: The shot had deadened the lower part of my body, from the bottom of my spine down through my legs. But my belly, where the contractions were taking place, was completely unaffected. I felt the immense pain of every single contraction.

What a relief—and what joy when my baby was born: We have a daughter—Rebecca Marie!

"And she's alive!" I felt enormous gratitude as I returned to my room, where my roommate was in shock and mourning.

The next morning, I awoke with an intense headache—the after-effect of the spinal. Dealing with the pain impacted the experience of pleasure and joy at the presence of the baby girl. I felt so angry at having been given the spinal.

Dr. Laird would never have done that, I thought. *They're so behind the times here in Texas!*

After a few days we drove back over the causeway to the mainland with our newborn, and introduced Rebecca Marie to Steve and Chris, who welcomed their baby sister with curiosity and enthusiasm.

Our expanded family life came with new experiences. While watching the boys play outdoors, I began a new—and short-lived—hobby of doing crewel embroidery as baby Rebecca lay in her playpen, her eyes following the playful actions of her brothers nearby.

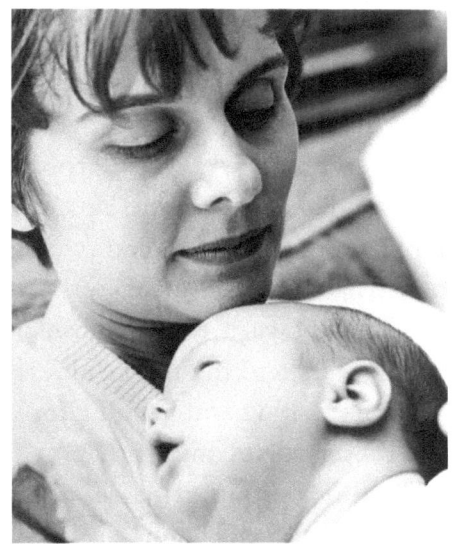

Rebecca Marie's birth

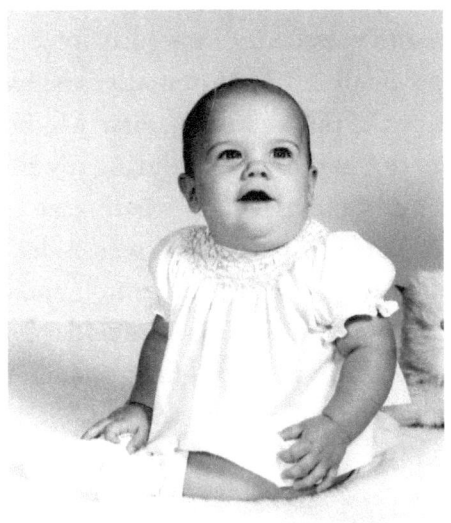

Becca

In the summer, the group of ministers and their wives who lived in our district and with whom we met periodically, decided to go on a camping trip. We were excited and curious to see how our newest family member would take to this. She did fine, sleeping well at night and appearing to enjoy the scenery. But there was a problem: I forgot to bring the diapers! (Believe it or not, this was before there were disposable ones available.) I had two dishcloths with me, and that's what became her diapers. After changing Becca, I would quickly wash the used dish cloth and hang it out to dry. So, thanks to my forgetfulness, I was pretty much tied up with washing and hanging for the remainder of our daughter's very first camping trip.

One couple in our group of pastors became our best friends: F.D. Dawson and Thelma Jean Goodrich. F.D. had graduated from Perkins Seminary at SMU. Thelma Jean graduated from SMU in 1962 and had been a Kappa Alpha Theta and president of the sorority. So, we had that in common, though during different years. Her father was Robert Goodrich, the pastor of First Methodist Church in Dallas where I had attended during my first year. (Her grandfather had held a revival meeting at our church in Nacogdoches when I was twelve. It was under his invitation that I walked down the aisle to the pulpit and dedicated my life to Christ.) F.D. and Thelma Jean had their first pastorate in a very small town not too far from us. And we found we had many things in common, including babies. (Their daughter, Dolly, and son, Davey, were just a bit younger than our boys.)

The Dawsons also were very concerned about the civil rights movement. When the Selma March was announced,

Walter and F.D. decided immediately to join it. They took off, and Thelma Jean and I were at home with our children, hoping and praying our husbands would return safe and sound. And they did, after a demanding, stressful, and deeply gratifying experience.

Years later, Thelma Jean and I would reconnect after many life changes, during her remarkable career as a professor and therapist at M.D. Anderson Medical School in Houston.

Back to New York, 1967

We had lived in Hitchcock for five years. The Bishop and his cabinet were not that fond of Walter. His outspokenness had annoyed them. They had refused to assign us to a Black church, as Walter had originally requested. And they weren't moving us anywhere. Walter was becoming restless. He had completed his dissertation and been awarded his doctorate. He began to wonder about looking for a teaching position in a seminary.

Then, out of the blue an amazing thing happened. Early one morning Walter received a phone call inviting him to join the New Testament department of Union Seminary! We couldn't believe it. My immediate response was: "And have my children's playground be on top of a *building*? No way!" But that concern rather quickly faded as we began to let in what this move would mean for our lives. By the afternoon, the answer was YES! Here we come, New York!

This time we packed up our household goods in a U-Haul trailer, hitched it up to our station wagon, and with great excitement started out for the City That Never

Becca and Calico

Settled in the Seminary

Sleeps. As we finally arrived in New Jersey and could see the New York skyline before us, we were speechless. *We're almost home!*

We moved into McGiffert Hall, where we had lived when Steve was born, but this time in a faculty apartment. It felt beyond imagination that we were no longer on the student side of things. In the five years we were away there had been changes. Walter met his New Testament colleague, Lou Martyn, who, along with his wife, Dot, and their sons, became close family friends.

The annual salary for an associate faculty member was $18,000. But there were additional benefits. Housing was free, and each child was awarded $3,000 yearly for private school. The boys entered Agnes Russell School at Columbia Teacher's College, just across the street. They loved their teachers and soon made many new friends. Becca joined other children her age—not on the roof, thankfully—but in a playroom with interesting things to do. At home, she was especially happy with her new kitty, Calico.

The kids also had seminary friends who were their age, children of faculty and students. The boys loved roaming the hallways, playing in the central garden area known as the quadrangle, and even having fun on the rooftop of McGiffert Hall.

A New Direction

Back in New York with three young kids, I wondered what part-time activity I could engage in. My longing to dance was still strong, but I could in no way become a professional dancer at my age, thirty-two, with no serious training.

Then I heard that there was something called *dance therapy*. What was that? I went to a four-day workshop on the East Side taught by Marian Chace, an elderly woman from a famous psychiatric hospital in D.C., who was considered the originator of dance therapy. I was thrilled and fascinated! (I was the least experienced person in the workshop.) At the end of the four days each attendee took a turn leading the group, utilizing what had been taught. And when it came my turn, I was extremely nervous. But I did my best, and felt enormous relief when it was done.

"Do, do, do!" Marian responded, an irritated look on her face. I was dumbfounded. Her reaction to my performance painfully activated what I would later call my "core wound": *My best is not good enough*. I broke into tears.

I learned that Marian Chace was not into "doing." She stressed the importance of seeing and feeling where the patient was, and responding accordingly. Although painful, it was a lesson to learn that was essential to the rest of my professional life.

I soon began to volunteer at Manhattan State Psychiatric Hospital one morning a week. The first time I arrived there, I sat in my car for a full half-hour, trying to control my anxiety and summon the courage to go inside. What was I *thinking*? Did I really want to go *inside* this formidable, mammoth building on Ward's Island . . . and do what? Teach crazy people to move therapeutically? Have *I* gone crazy? Finally, I opened the car door and slowly walked to the entrance.

I was led up to the seventh floor by the lovely volunteer (who lived next to Jackie Kennedy on Fifth Avenue), and into a large spare room. There was a circle of chairs filled by empty-faced men, with several attendants standing in the background.

Manhattan State Psychiatric Hospital

"This is Virginia Wink, gentlemen. She's here to lead you in dance therapy." They were silent, expressionless. I walked over to the record player on a nearby table and put on some music. I sat down, hoping my trembling was not too visible, and took a deep breath. The voice of Marian Chace was in my head:

"Feel the energy in the room. Tune in to the patients. What small, peripheral movements do you see? Hands or feet moving? Begin there. Start with the smallest movement, and gradually develop it to include other, and finally all, parts of the body."

The seemingly immobile men began, one after another, to follow the movements that their bodies suggested to me. The music gradually changed from slow and quiet to more lively. After a while everyone was standing, arms were waving, and the circle moved around the room. There were expressions on faces now, a verbal wisecrack here and there, even occasional laughter. At the end of an hour I brought things to a quiet close.

"I'll see you here next week," I said. There was gentle applause.

After a time, my volunteer day at Manhattan State vaulted into a full-time job. I moved from the adult wards to the Children's Treatment Center. I loved working with children and young people, and I became good friends with the other adults in the field who were employed there. (One particularly close friend was Jane Downs Cathcart, a truly talented and dynamic woman. We would remain in touch for years to come, and eventually came to refer to each other as "sister.") Before I took a break when we went to California for Walter's sabbatical, I drafted a proposal for altering and adding to the structure of our programs, such as involving the staff members in activities with the children. Some, not all, of the suggestions were put to use while I was away.

Meanwhile, I had also discovered another form of movement training, taught by an amazing woman from South Wales. Betty Meredith-Jones had been a protégé of Rudolph Laban, an Austro-Hungarian dance artist. She taught Laban effort-shape movement analysis at New School and Columbia Teacher's College, as well as classes at Riverside Church. I joined half a dozen women who were in an apprenticeship with Betty, and for four or more years we had about five hours a week of movement training. Our group became very good friends, and we loved our work with Betty. One of the women was Eileen Jones—also originally from Great Britain—with whom I would remain in contact.

As time went by I became a member of the American Dance Therapy Association. One weekend I attended a conference where the speaker was Alexander Lowen, MD, a psychiatrist and founder of the International Institute for Bioenergetic Analysis. Lowen had been a student of Wilhelm Reich, who had been ousted from the inner circle of Sigmund Freud because of his emphasis on including the body and sexuality in diagnosing and treating mental illness.

In his speech, Lowen wowed the crowd of dance therapists with his energy and enthusiasm, as well as his theory. Encouraged in his presentation by the rapt audience, Lowen was vibrant and appealing. He seemed unlike any therapist I had ever seen. I left the meeting resolved to be his patient.

It took me a year to get up the courage to call Lowen's office. When I did I found he had no openings in his schedule. I was referred to a woman, Hazel Stanley, one of the very few women connected to the Institute at that time, and worked with her for a year. Then finally Dr. Lowen had an hour available at his home office in New Canaan, Connecticut. I happily drove that fifty miles and back on alternating Fridays, until finally I was able to see him in his New York office.

My time with Al Lowen was lifesaving. A major focus of his work was the physical expression of anger which, according to his theory, was essential to mental health; major illnesses, physical and mental, were caused and exacerbated by the suppression of anger, which was locked in the body. I was given a tennis racket and instructed to bang it onto a pillow over and over while shrieking the words that came to mind. Nothing could have been farther from my life experience! And nothing could have felt better. He also had me stand firm and pound my fists, shouting, "I have a *right*!" To be free. To be my true self.

Through my dance therapy experience I had found the person whose theory and practice would change my life in ways I had not imagined possible.

The Inner Journey:
The Search for the True Self

During the first decade of married life, I experienced many happy occasions—above all, the births of our three children. Our external life was engrossing, often satisfying, and sometimes joyful. But there was another level, not outwardly apparent, that was manifesting on an inward—and mostly silent—level.

The following notes were written in the spring of 1964, while living in Hitchcock, Texas. They reflect the early stages of my inner journey.

A breathing spell. Transition. I am grateful for the realization which came only yesterday that the incredible inner turbulence of the past few months was largely due to the awakening of the life-long desire for freedom. Everyone talks of freedom these days. The Black person says, I want my freedom. I nod and say <u>yes</u>. The South African says, We want *freedom. We say Yes. Others ask. Yes, Yes. But has it been two years ago when Henry Elkin [my Jungian analyst in NYC] asked me, "What is it that you want?" How could I understand the answer that came struggling upward, having been lying asleep in a deep secret place: "Freedom." Once uttered, how frightening! But once uttered, never to sleep again. Fear banishes it, uncertainty curses it, anxiety throttles it. But this wish, this desire, this vision survives, and awaits understanding.*

Little did I know that Freedom would come in the form of reexamining my anger, my Christian faith, and the relationship between the two.

The following words were written around the same time, apparently in response to a request to speak about my life and views regarding the church:

I was born in a minister's family, and grew up loving the church and being very serious about the faith. We had a close, happy family, but I think we would all agree now that there were a couple of things we would change if we could. First, we were very conscious of how we <u>ought</u> to act and live as Christians and as a minister's family. This "ought" lay so heavily upon us that we tended to repress or disregard those human aspects of our individual personalities or our life together which contradicted the ought, rather than accepting and dealing with them openly. One such negative aspect was <u>anger</u>. According to our perspective at that *time, anger was not a Christian virtue, so it was not expressed or confessed: It was stored. We "ought" not to be angry!*

Two important needs had much to do with shaping my personality and my attitude toward the Christian faith and life in general. As far back as I can remember, I had the strong desire for the freedom to be exactly who I was, for better or for worse, without any reference to someone else's expectation of me. This was, in large part, a built-in rebellion against the <u>ought</u>, but I believe it was also a genuine longing for <u>authentic being</u>.

The second was a very great need for acceptance and approval among my peers, and especially among the good Christian people within the churches we served. Most of the time the need for approval won out.

These needs were in conflict, because one cannot be authentic and <u>real</u> when the desire for acceptance leads one, as it inevitably does, to conforming to the opinions of others.

I went away to college being certain that what I wanted most of all was to marry a minister and continue the kind of life I had always lived. I hadn't been there but a few days when I spotted the one beside which there were no others, and three years later we were married. Shortly after we moved to New York City.

This was a big change for us, to say the very least. It marked the end of a rather protected, provincial, predictable existence. With the move we had come into an expanding universe which every day brought its new experiences, its revised understandings, and its baffling complexities.

For me, one of the most important experiences—and most painful—came in our first year, through a couple of religion courses I took, taught by the wife of a renowned theologian, Reinhold Niebuhr. Through examining the religious phenomenon in America as a whole, I came to feel that my own serious, pious religious faith had its roots in this need for acceptance and approval, that it had been self-centered, and had failed to arouse in me a real working concern for my neighbor in the broadest sense, and therefore had missed the point of the Christian gospel. By the time I took the final examination, I had pretty well written off my religious experience of the past. I have no doubt now that much which was valid and real was discarded, along with what was immature and erroneous. But I have only gratitude for that experience, for it has meant growth that couldn't have come any other way.

After our fifth year in New York we spent the summer in a small rural pastorate in Texas before returning for our final year at the seminary. For several months I was back in the parsonage, and this time as the parson's wife with two small sons as "PKs." I began to experience a rather vague sense of anxiety, which followed me back to New York in the fall. I finally realized that being in the parish again had activated within me the battle of the needs: freedom vs. approval. Six years in New

York City, six years of being neither preacher's daughter nor preacher's wife, but merely a _person_, had strengthened this desire for freedom. So the battle raged. It was then that I realized just to what extent I _had_ been enslaved by the image and the command of the _ought_. And suddenly the prospect of returning to the old milieu of the parsonage, the parish, and the conference seemed unbearable.

I couldn't bear to have to conform to this arbitrary, unreal image, but deep inside was fear of the criticism, the lack of acceptance if I did not. I spent that last year in intensive soul-searching and "psyche-searching," in an effort to resolve this conflict, and in an all-out quest for inner freedom and an understanding of who I really was. [This was experienced largely through my therapy with Henry Elkin and his therapy group.] The more I discovered, the less I wanted to return to life in the parish. But we did return, with me inwardly kicking and screaming. It seemed to me that I was leaving behind my real home.

We moved to Hitchcock, Texas. It WAS a contrast! I had moved around a great deal all my life and never had had difficulty adjusting to a new environment. But to say I had difficulty now was to understate. I felt that if God had been in the recent circumstances of my life, he had played a dirty trick on me. Here I'd gone to a lot of trouble to discover who I was, to be a real person, and now I was in a situation in which I thought I couldn't be free to BE that person. Everything seemed out of kilter, and I was miserable.

I also had serious questions about the church. I didn't see much evidence that it was mediating the transformation either of the corporate evils of society or of the private hells of individuals. I felt it was creating mine. Why, if the church made no significant difference in a person's life, couldn't we just go off, live our own lives, and work for brotherhood of man and peace on earth through far less cumbersome channels? That would certainly have made life easier for me!

When I expressed such thoughts as these, I hardly got a pat on the back from our colleagues in the ministry. And I was hardly supportive of my husband. My attitudes were a burden to him. I knew this, and I felt very guilty about it and the whole conflict I was in. Therefore, I tried to keep those feelings to myself. I was left alone with my inner demons of resentment and guilt, and felt quite cut off from everyone. And soon the "demons" began to produce periods of depression and acute anxiety.

Needless to say, my therapy with Dr. Alexander Lowen, with its emphasis on the mind/body connection, the expression of feelings (particularly anger), was for me a Godsend. There was another world out there which called to me.

That world of Bioenergetic therapy added depth and meaning to my work as a dance therapist. And it offered a new understanding of the world I had grown up in, as well as a different and new way to be a part of it. In that context the longing for freedom didn't seem such an outlandish or impossible desire. And it provided the support as well as the possibility for achieving that goal. It also invited a new perspective regarding the experience and expression of anger.

We spent the summer of 1971 in the small town of Phillips, Maine, where Walter served as visiting pastor at the local Methodist Church. While he was away one Sunday, I took his place and gave the sermon. It was clearly a reflection of the work I had been doing in my therapy with Alexander Lowen.

Below is a revised version of the sermon.

EPH. 4:25-27

"Therefore, putting away falsehood, let everyone speak the truth with his neighbor, for we are members one of another. Be angry but do not sin; do not let the sun go down on your anger, and give no opportunity to the devil."

What I want to discuss this morning is an area which concerns me deeply: dealing with anger.

Inability to deal with anger is mixed up with a lot of illness. At the hospital where I work I see people who have held inside great stores of anger until they either explode in uncontrollable, aggressive behavior, or their efforts to hold it down deplete all energy so that they become immobilized by depression. Sometimes the anger is turned in on themselves and they become suicidal. Most of us don't get to such extreme states. But most of us suffer in many ways because we don't know how to handle anger. We experience mild depressions, chronic tension, aches and pains of all kinds—and sometimes serious physical illness.

We allow small grievances, daily irritations, and insults—real and imagined—build between friends until we are enemies. We allow the sun to go down many times without dealing with our anger. And "the devil gets a foothold." We must find ways of dealing daily with our anger.

Perhaps being able to be more honest is the first step. But obviously we can't go around ranting and raving all the time, saying everything that pops into our minds. Someone has said that expressing anger adds guilt to our bad feelings. We need to learn to <u>confess it rather than express it</u>. There is a difference. We can delay our reactions long enough to cool off, reflect upon them, then go—before the sun sets, if possible, and confess the feelings to the person involved, and <u>talk it all out</u>.

What about the anger of children? Some of us today are carrying around anger that we felt as children when we were punished unjustly, when we were misunderstood or ridiculed, when our needs went unmet. In the name of respect to elders, children are not allowed an outlet for their very deep feelings of anger. For the sake of their health and stability we must be willing to differentiate between impudent back-talk and needed expression of anger and resentment toward us, their parents or relatives. We need to structure into family life a time for private talks—opportunities for angry feelings to surface and be communicated "before the sun sets."

Obviously, we all experience some anger which we simply cannot express toward the person or persons involved. It can be very helpful and very important to talk about it, get it off our chest to someone—to the minister or to a friend.

That phrase, "Getting it off our chest," is very apt. Because we do experience that anger inside our bodies. We don't <u>feel</u> in our heads. We <u>think</u> in our heads and <u>feel</u> in our bodies. That's why our bodies suffer so much from pent-up emotions. Talking it over with someone can bring great relief, both physically and emotionally.

But the body itself can help tremendously with this problem of dealing with anger. I work part of the time with boys between the ages of six to twelve. When two of them begin an angry exchange of curse words or start hitting each other or throwing furniture, I hand them a bean bag and challenge them to hit the clown that's painted on the wall. Or I have them pound on a drum. Or we go stomping or jumping around the room in rhythm to rock and roll music. We don't tell them to shut up nor force them to sit still in a chair. We give them an alternative method of expressing their feelings.

With a group of adult patients, whose feelings of anger are not nearly so apparent, what may begin as rhythmic tapping of the feet progresses into very strong stamping, or pushing into the middle of the circle with fists. This is fun and even funny to the participants. But a lot of aggressive energy is released and dissipated that way. It is an alternative to verbal and physical fights. We can *all learn from that. <u>We all need to develop good physical outlets for stored-up anger.</u>*

As we grow older, we must continue to find ways in which we can be <u>physically active and physically expressive of our feelings of anger</u>. Many of the people I work with are in their 70s and 80s. Exercise and rhythmic movement is terribly important for them. They find that they are a lot more lively than they thought they could be. And the more active they are, the better they feel, physically and emotionally.

We must accept ourselves and each other as people who feel anger and resentment, who are capable of experiencing the whole range of human emotions from very good to very bad. We must learn to talk out our disputes and hurt feelings and work through disagreements. We must become more honest and more accepting so that we can therefore help each other to become more real, more authentic. That, I believe, is what the Christian community is all about. For only when we have learned to accept and deal with our anger are we truly free to give and receive love in full measure.

Clearly, this message to the congregation that Sunday came from my experience in therapy that had so powerfully impacted my life. It was a sermon to *myself*, a reminder to continue to learn how to recognize, accept, and deal with my own anger.

I'm still learning.

Travel Adventures

Noni, as the grandchildren called my mother, loved to travel. Dad was quite happy to stay at home and fish. After he retired at the early age of sixty-five, the two of them took several cruises and other trips with friends. Mother wanted more, and one way she got it was through her decision to take each of her grandchildren on a faraway trip when they turned eleven. (At that time, airfare for children was half-price before they reached twelve years of age.) Steve, as the oldest grandchild, was the first to experience such an adventure.

Mother planned to take Steve on a trip to Europe, and she invited me to come along. My eighty-year-old grandmother, Mam-ma, was also joining us. It was a grand trip, with the first stop in Amsterdam. Then Paris.

We arrived at an elegant hotel, across the street from the Paris Opera House. That night for dinner Steve and I were excited to have *escargot* for the first time. But, as the evening wore on, we both became ill and began throwing up. (We were the only ones sick—and the only ones who

Virginia Wink Hilton | 95

Grandmother trip

had eaten *escargot*!) After a couple of miserable hours late into the night, the two of us went out on our balcony that overlooked the Opera House. We breathed in the fresh night air, and then Steve began to talk.

"Mom, I had a bad dream. A man in a white suit came in and he was going to hurt me.," he said. He began to cry.

"I think you are dreaming about what happened in the hospital after your burn experience. That was a horrible time for you," I said, as I held him tightly. It was the first time we had verbally referenced that trauma that had occurred when he was fifteen months old. I was enormously relieved and grateful for the opportunity to do so. We talked about that traumatic experience for a while, and then went back to our beds and slept the rest of the night.

The next morning we were scheduled for a bus tour to Montmartre. Steve and I were both weak and a bit shaky from our nighttime experience. But we didn't want to miss the tour. So we got on the bus, hoping we could tolerate the drive.

We arrived at Montmartre and the bus parked on the street. I was strongly feeling the need for a restroom. I got off the bus, leaving Steve with his grandmother, and I asked a policeman on the corner where I could find a restroom. He waved me off in French, not understanding my request in English. I felt a bit of panic. A middle-aged man who was standing close by motioned to me to follow him. The urgency I was dealing with gave me no choice but to do so. He crossed the street and then went into an alley. I followed. It was completely empty. After a brisk walk of several hundred feet he slowed down, looked back at me, and pointed to a door in what looked like a shed. As I started toward it, he reached in his pocket and handed me a couple of tissues. I went inside. There was nothing there except a hole in the floor! I awkwardly straddled the hole and got relief.

Now what do I do? I wondered. Nearby there was a heavy cord hanging from the ceiling. I pulled on it. Water came bubbling up from the floor, soaking my feet, and then disappeared. I was relieved but terrified. What will that man do when I come out? I took a deep breath and slowly opened the creaking door. There was no one there. The alley was completely empty. I hurried back to the bus—feeling relief all around!

Finally, Mother's sister, Ann, at that time the principal of the American School for Armed Forces Dependents in Germany, met us in her Mercedes-Benz and drove us to her home near Bitburg. We had a delightful evening with the family who were Aunt Ann's neighbors, and were treated to an enormous array of typical German cuisine. The house was built over a small barn, where there was a cow and a huge vat of sauerkraut. For years after, Steve would remember the intense smell that permeated the house.

The next day we drove to Darmstadt where my younger brother Bill was a First Lieutenant, B Battery Commander in the 3rd Battalion, 80th Artillery. We then went on to Pfundstadt, where Bill lived, and we all enjoyed a leisurely visit with him. (It was during the Vietnam War, and, needless to say, we were so grateful that he had been sent to Germany rather than to the war zone.)

After that Aunt Ann drove us back down through Bavaria, with a stop in Salzburg for a marvelous Mozart concert. Somewhere along the way we began commenting on the great ride we were having in the Mercedes. Someone asked Aunt Ann if she had a name for her fancy automobile. No, she didn't. We began a lively conversation, trying to come up with the right name for the car. Meanwhile, Mam-ma was slumped over, chin on her chest, sound asleep . . . or so we thought. Then someone asked, "Well, is this Mercedes a boy or a girl?"

"It's a boy," Mam-ma muttered, eyes still closed. "It's got nuts."

We were astounded—and couldn't stop laughing! Our dear grandmother was totally prim and proper, very quiet most of the time. On a rare occasion she would surprise us with an unusual comment. This one I certainly could never forget! I don't recall whether Aunt Ann decided on a name. But with her at the wheel, the "boy" took us around and, later, got us to the plane for our flight back home.

What a special time it had been for all of us!

* * *

In 1971, as summer approached, we longed for a change of scenery and an adventure. That was when Walter took the job of guest pastor at a church in the small town of Phillips, Maine. The children were excited over the opportunity to explore and enjoy nature, as were their parents.

A highlight of the summer was a hike on nearby Saddleback Mountain. We left Rebecca with the next-door neighbors, hoping they would take good care of her, while we headed out with our backpacks stocked for the overnight excursion. The boys were good hikers, and we loved the climb, the views, and our time together. As we neared the summit it was time to set up our tent for the night. We crammed into the sleeping bags, and managed a decent night's sleep. The next morning, as we were packing up, a hiker passing by noticed that our leftover food had been stored at the head of our sleeping bags. "You're lucky a bear didn't sniff out that food and come in after it!" he shouted. Oh, dear. Walter and I looked at each other in alarm, realizing how stupid we had been.

As we continued the hike the sky became overcast, and soon there were snow flurries that completely obscured our vision.

"It's snowing!" the boys shouted with enormous excitement. "And it's the middle of summer!"

As the snowfall subsided we made our way back down the mountain, and our path ended near Rangeley, Maine. Somewhat weary but happy about our adventure, we went back to our summer home to embrace our missing family member, Rebecca.

Shortly after our hike, Walter left for a week in California. He had become interested in a retreat center named Four Springs in Napa Valley, established by Elizabeth Howes, a Jungian analyst and founder of the Guild for Psychological Studies. He decided to attend a retreat there to learn about her approach, which combined "depth psychology and the teachings of Jesus, religious studies, mythology, and experiential learning." His experience during that time would be the beginning of a powerful change in his life.

After I had delivered the sermon at the church in Phillips while Walter was away, I began to feel a yearning to get "on the road again." I approached the children: "How would you like to drive over to the coast and go camping overnight?" They were excited. We packed up our gear and some food supplies and started out for Bar Harbor.

"The people here in Maine say, 'Bah Hobbuh.' Sounds like Bah Humbug!" Steve joked as we entered the town. We drove onto Mt. Desert Island and into Acadia National Park. Soon we found a great camping spot and began to unload our gear. Steve and Chris, ages thirteen and ten, set up the tent for Rebecca and me, and the pup tent for the two of them. The children spent the rest of the daylight hours happily exploring the area around our campsite. After our evening meal they continued playing together in the light of the campfire, while I stretched out on the lounge chair that we brought with us. As I watched them, feeling much satisfaction and joy about how our adventure was proceeding, the thought came into my head: *I can do this. I can do this by myself!* I was surprised—startled, even—at such unexpected words. Words that came from the mostly unconscious process that was slowly gathering inside me.

We settled into our tents and went to sleep. But in the middle of the night, quite suddenly there were strong winds and a deluge of rain. After a few minutes I realized that our tents wouldn't keep us dry much longer. I scrambled out of my sleeping bag and went to the pup tent.

"Wake up, Steve! Wake up, Chris! It's raining and we have to get things back into the car—quickly!" Steve got the food items in the trunk, while I settled five-year-old Rebecca into the back seat. Chris was sound asleep and not easily aroused. Steve had to drag him out into the pouring rain. But, finally we were all safe and sound—and dry—inside the car.

When morning came the rain had moved on, and we managed to have a sufficient breakfast before leaving our camp site. Down the road we were able to join a group of tourists and a park ranger who pointed out and educated us on the sea life that surrounded us. Eventually we stopped at a fish market and purchased a lobster to take back to Phillips for Walter's homecoming the next day. On the drive home I felt enormous relief—and pride—over the fact that our adventure had gone so well. And I felt an inner validation of my personal capacity to take care of my children—alone.

California, Here We Come!

Walter was to have a sabbatical leave during the spring semester and summer of 1972. For many months we had planned to spend the time in Germany, as was customary for New Testament scholars. But due to a quirk of fate all plans changed.

The trip to Four Springs had been so impactful for Walter that he wanted more of what was offered there. So, in January we left New York to spend seven months in California.

Our station wagon was packed full. The boys spent most of the time stretched out across the sleeping bags that covered suitcases and other paraphernalia, and Becca sat between us. We had a fun time rolling through the countryside—woods, plains, mountains, valleys, deserts. Finally, we arrived in the Golden State—to begin what was a golden time for us, and the beginning of many changes.

Former seminary friends graciously welcomed us and helped us settle in Berkeley, where we quickly fell in love with the entire Bay Area, its beauty and its way of life. We moved into a small cottage in the Berkeley flats. Steve and Chris enrolled in the nearby public school, often getting roughed up on their way in and out of classes each day.

Shortly before Easter we had the extreme good fortune to move into a house that was a New York apartment-dweller's paradise: a lovely home high in the Oakland hills, in a pine forest where deer roamed freely. We spent much of our days soaking up the sunshine and absorbing the incredible beauty of the lush flowering plants and trees, as well as enjoying a quiet that was rarely broken except for the songs of birds. The children enjoyed their greater freedom, the safer public schools, and the many close friendships they developed. Next door to us was a family with two young teenaged daughters, and that was a boon for Steve and Chris. Becca made fast friends with the girl across the street.

For Walter and me the time was meaningful and productive far beyond expectations. For him, the intensive training with the Guild for Psychological Studies was highly rewarding. It brought him into a new method of teaching New Testament, which was what he had been reaching after for a long time. And he wrote a short book, entitled *The Bible and Human Transformation*, that was soon widely read.

I was able to continue my current interests by teaching body movement classes at Montclair Presbyterian Church in Oakland. And I began sessions with a Bioenergetic therapist.

In my Christmas letter the following December I wrote:

A hiatus from routine involvements, frantic schedules, the inevitable fracturing of energy and interests . . . The opportunity to withdraw, reflect, and regroup.

The exhilarating experience of focusing only on what one chooses as most important. I think time will prove it a kind of watershed for both of us.

And so it did.

At Montclair Presbyterian, the minister and church members welcomed my classes, and on Easter Sunday they invited me to lead a movement exercise for the entire congregation. I chose "Morning Has Broken," by Cat Stevens as the background for the movement. The title became the theme of the Easter service.

Almost everyone in the congregation joined in the movement with interest and enthusiasm, and some became regular members of the classes I taught weekly.

In the sixties and seventies there were drastic changes taking place in our culture. California was a bit ahead of the curve. So when we arrived there in 1972, there was a lot to adjust to.

Attitudes and activities were shifting radically in two areas: feminism and sexuality. Women in California were going without their bras, and couples were exploring open marriage. It was as if the lid had been taken off the bottled-up erotic needs and impulses of generations past. There was certainly something both exhilarating and disorienting about the atmosphere, the dynamic.

Wilhelm Reich, who was imprisoned during the McCarthy era and died there, had focused on the importance of sexuality, orgastic potency, and sexual freedom. In 1956 six tons of his books were burned at the Gansevoort Incinerator in New York City. Yet the social movements that occurred ten to twenty years after Reich's death—the human potential movement, the women's movement, and the so-called sexual revolution—were all heavily influenced by his writing. He believed that repressed sexuality was the source of many ills, including passivity in the face of authoritarianism, conflict of all sorts, and perverse and violent acts.

Reich, however, also believed in the importance—the necessity—of what he called "serial monogamy." When there was no longer love, sexual attraction, and satisfaction in a marriage, both persons should move on. But only one sexual relationship at a time.

In the sixties and seventies numerous couples who felt liberated by the sexual revolution jumped into the adventures—and trials and tribulations—of open marriage: "We're married, but we sleep with whomever we want!" This was the atmosphere that we landed in when we arrived in California.

I know of only one marriage from those days which survived that practice.

Before we left New York, Hazel Stanley had recommended that while I was in California I should see the highly regarded Stanley Keleman to continue Bioenergetic therapy. When I contacted him he said he had no openings at that time, and he referred me to Earl Cramer. I wrote to Hazel regarding my relationship with Cramer:

June 17, 1972

I was very disappointed at first [not to be able to see Keleman], but it seemed one of those synchronous happenings (which keep occurring to us out here in

California) that Earl was 1) an MD, which because of my insurance relieved our financial situation considerably, and 2) he, like me, was born the child of a Methodist minister! It meant an instant bond between us—lots of early experiences in common, many attitudes and reactions shaped by the same or similar influences. Earl happens to be about the opposite of Walter in every way. The chief thing, though, is that he's very much a <u>feeling</u> person, with a gentle, tender, caring quality that whenever I've encountered it in a man during the last couple of years, I've responded with a flood of tears (inwardly if not actually) and longing.

In the course of the therapy I've gotten to feelings of longing—of reaching—of there being nobody there, that I'm certain go back to infancy. Some very important, crucial experiences. Much of the rest of the time and energy have been spent in fighting against the negative feelings and conflicts surrounding the marriage and the situation as already described. And then finally allowing it all to surface. (Or it seems like <u>all</u>.) And now where am I? At the moment on the feeling level—kind of bruised, and hurting, and weary. Lots of tears, and lots more to come. The next thing, I know, is the <u>anger</u>. One hell of a lot of it in the right now. And then all that anger that's been trapped forever.

And then, coping with the dissatisfactions of which I am now fully aware. I feel bewildered by that. But Walter and I are talking now. Sometimes in the past we've talked and shared unwisely, but at least we know how to communicate, and that has been the cornerstone of the relationship. Also, Walter has been in analysis with a woman (Jungian) therapist and apparently has really covered a lot of ground. Incredibly enough (or maybe not so incredible), about the time I would bring up in my therapy an area in the relationship or something specifically about him that was problematic for me, he would have a dream about it and it would become an open issue in his therapy. So—the can of worms has been opened from both ends. . . .

The therapy with Earl Cramer set in motion my thoughts and concerns regarding sexual feelings and responses in the therapeutic setting. Some years later those subjects would be explored in speeches and articles on transference and countertransference, and ultimately would appear in a doctoral dissertation.

During our months in northern California, Walter spent a number of days at Four Springs, learning from his new mentor, Elizabeth Howes. Every aspect of his life was being impacted by what he was experiencing through her guidance.

While it was so meaningful and important to me to continue my work in Bioenergetic Analysis through the sessions with Earl Cramer, I was also very pleased when the time came for me to go to Four Springs for a weekend retreat. I was very familiar with Jungian analysis from my days of working with Henry Elkin in New York. But Elizabeth Howes and her colleagues had devised a unique program that involved art, movement, and meditation, as well as Biblical scripture.

It was during the retreat at Four Springs that the powerful, iconic image emerged: the butterfly with scissors at its wings. Another image that surfaced was the cracked face of my very first doll, left in the sand pile during a rainy night, which was, no doubt, my first experience of grief.

While the weekend at Four Springs had been quite significant and pleasurable for me, when the time came to go there a second time, I found myself in conflict. There was a Bioenergetic conference scheduled at the same time at Satori, a retreat center in the mountains below San Francisco. My therapy work, with emphasis on the body and the expression of feeling, was so very exciting and impactful for me, and I wanted more. I chose to go to Satori.

This decision was a huge disappointment for Walter. And it was for me the beginning of new behavior: making a decision on behalf of my own needs and desires—even when it was in conflict with his.

Along with the serious activities that engaged us, we had many fun and pleasurable times during our months in California. We had a lot of friends during our stay, many new, and a few we had known in New York. One such person was John Pearson, who had been at Union Seminary but then moved to Berkeley. He was a photographer whose most famous work is "The Little Girl on the Beach." His book of photographs, *Kiss the Joy As It Flies*, had been published several years before.

John Pearson's publisher was Don Gerard, who started the very successful New Age publishing company, Book Works. One of the special gifts to me during those months in California was the relationship with Don and his wife Eugenia. Don was an artistic person, always creating something new—and very different. Eugenia was a woman with a loving heart, and it soon became clear to me that she was a soul mate. When we first met, she was working with seniors in Berkeley and later became a psychotherapist. Our friendship would last until her death from cancer in 2010.

* * *

In August of 1972, we had to face the sad reality that our sabbatical in California was coming to an end. In planning for our return to New York, we decided a new car would be a better transport than our old station wagon. We bought an Audi, and then realized it wasn't big enough to carry all of us *and* our expanded belongings. So, we decided, Walter and the boys would drive cross-country, and Becca and I would fly home. Steve and Chris, sad to say goodbye to the Oakland Hills and all of California, were nonetheless excited about their boys-only trip. Becca and I took the several days before our flight to prepare the house and grounds for our departure—and the return of the homeowners.

Here are my exasperated words written on the plane that was to take us back to New York:

Mutterings from a 747 . . . Sept. 2, 1972

The plane is grounded—and I'm not. For some reason known only to God and American Airlines, this winged monster won't go. It's 4:00 p.m. (scheduled leaving time was 1:00 p.m.) and they're replacing something. Very consoling. "They" are trying to make me happy by plying me with complimentary alcohol. But it's just making me bitchy. I feel rather like I'm stuck in purgatory.

Fortunately, Becca has a friend on the other side of her seat—a young high school girl who blessedly likes kids, and is doing a kind of origami with Juicy Fruit wrappers.

So I thought I'd deal with my anxiety by writing.

The last night—and morning—(and afternoon!) in California have really been something! I finished scrubbing the bottom of the last pot at about 2 a.m. I fell into bed, trusting my luck to awaken in time to get the last four hundred bricks in place by the light of day. I was awakened by a meow at 2:45. A meow! I thought I had just gone ahead and freaked. But there was Agnes (the neighbor's cat), who comes around quite often, but who never gets invited in. After a few frantic moments I discovered an open kitchen window—opened last night by a benevolent (?) neighbor who was demonstrating her super-efficient oven cleaner. (The open window was to keep us from asphyxiating on oven-cleaner fumes.) I never open that window. And never once did I think of closing it. So Agnes spent the night with us—which might have been okay—except she couldn't wait and pissed all over the big silk pillows on the floor in the living room.

My friend, Connie, came in time to pull us together and into her car—at 11:30 a.m. Late, we thought, to get to the airport in time for the one o'clock departure. At the last minute I remembered the hanging clothes bag, unlocked the door and chain, and added it to our overweight. On the way out I saw the mailman who was yelling at me about a change of address. I got distracted, thinking I'd go back inside with any mail for the owners. Then I got frantic about the time. We can't miss that plane! We drove off, and Connie asked, after a couple of minutes, if I wanted to stop two seconds to think if I'd left anything. No.—Yes, God! We roared back. The front door was left wide open! The only time I've flown today (when I should be winging over Des Moines, Iowa about now) was on the way to that door and back. Now during these cozy hours inside this damn 747, I'm absolutely haunted by the fear that Agnes went back to look for her silky substitute for a litter box and was sniffing around the living room when I turned the key, sealing her doom.

The thought of the sight and smell awaiting the owners when they return on September 18th to discover a disintegrating Agnes—sends me after another dreadful gin and tonic. –Cheers!

Finally, Rebecca and I made it home safely. So did the boys. (And we learned that Agnes had not been trapped in the house after all!)

Expansion

Christmas Letter, December 1972:

[We are] still readjusting to being back in New York City, determined to keep alive and aware, in spite of the daily assault on the senses of screeching brakes and sirens, the proliferated graffiti that seems an outcry against isolation and anonymity, the filth in the air. Determined not to become again exhausted and drained and divided by too many worthwhile involvements. . . . Where do we hope to be? Growing. Each of us has hopes and plans for the next few years which will be underway by the time we write again.

Clearly our time in California—the atmosphere, the climate, the environment, friends and experiences—had made such an impact. We came home different people. And we had major changes to look forward to.

The boys returned to their schools: Steve to Dalton, and first -grader Becca joined Chris at Agnes Russell, Columbia Teacher's College. Walter resumed his busy teaching schedule at the Seminary. I returned to my job at Manhattan Children's Treatment Center on Ward's Island and resumed my therapy with Al Lowen. I also began a night class at Columbia School of Social Work, with the aim of being accepted into the master's program. We were again back to busy lives in New York City.

Before we left California, to our total surprise and amazement, we received word from Union Seminary that an apartment had become available for us in Knox Hall. During the late sixties, about the time we returned from Texas, riots and protests were taking place at Columbia University, and Union students joined in. One area of focus was bringing equality to seminary housing. Knox Hall was the ultimate, elegant housing for faculty. In the '20s or '30s it had been designed grandly to help attract the star theologians from Europe. The protesters pressured the administration to determine availability based on family size rather than faculty status. While we were away the head of the music department retired, and his apartment became available. Our three children put us at the top of the list.

Soon after the family reunited in New York, we began preparing for our move to Knox Hall. When we walked into our new home-to-be we were simply speechless! Opening the brass door, we stepped into the foyer, which was itself the size of many New York apartments. On the first floor there were two large living rooms, a dining room, a large kitchen and laundry room, and two small servants' bedrooms with a bath. A hand-carved staircase led to the second floor, where there was a family room in the center of four bedrooms and two baths. Unbelievable!

Walter and I did a good bit of shopping to decorate our new home. We were fortunate to find a slightly used grand piano at a very good price from a seller in Brooklyn. And we had two beanbag sofas made out of Persian rugs for our second living room—just a little hippy touch in the midst of all the elegance.

For the first time the boys had their own bedrooms. They were thrilled. And Becca felt like a princess with a room spacious enough to include all her dolls and toys. The master bedroom and bath, overlooking the quadrangle, needless to say was large and comfortable. We would be living like royalty—at a theological seminary!

California—Again!

At some point during that year the decision was made to return to Berkeley for the '73 summer break. We had received an invitation from Eugenia and Don Gerard to house-sit their beautiful and comfortable home in Berkeley for the summer. Don was selling his publishing company, and the two of them had decided to buy a boat and sail around Hawaii. All five of us were thrilled to be returning to California. For me, it was like responding to my soul's call to return to its rightful home.

As during our first time in California, we had many pleasant family experiences and adventures, both traveling to-and-from, and while staying in the Gerards' home. The boys enjoyed reconnecting with friends from the year before. And Becca was happy to find several girls in the new neighborhood who became roller skating buddies.

At the same time, there was strain and stress between Walter and me, emanating mostly from my "inner journey"— my own inner need for freedom. I wrote the following:

It seems that feelings of wanting separation—not just in the psychic sense—but in a very real, total way—i.e., the dissolution of the marriage—was a part of the search for my own freedom—and the lost parts of myself. It seemed that progress, the road out, was also the road away, chiefly because of the connections between Walter and my mother, and between Walter and the moralistic, religious environment: two constricting, imprisoning aspects of my life.

Clearly, in my personal therapy with Al Lowen I had been working on my relationship with my parents, and my mother in particular. For most of my life, with few exceptions, I experienced fully my love, my gratitude, and my admiration for my mother. But at that time, the suppressed negativity, anger, and pain were bubbling to the surface. And clearly my connection to Walter and his behavior was complicating and complicated by my relationship to Mother. In order to get out of the "prison," I felt, I needed time apart.

My friend Connie, who lived in San Francisco, was going to be away for a few weeks. When I shared with her my desire to have some alone-time, she offered her apartment. This felt to me like a dream come true. Walter felt differently, but we agreed to the separation for most of the summer. He would be back at Four Springs for several weeks, so we would take turns being with the kids.

During this time I wrote the following letter to Al Lowen:

Dear Al,

I have been in California for a month now, and so many important things have happened already that I'd like to bring you up to date.

After we arrived here I told Walter I wanted a separation for the summer. He countered with all kinds of arguments, chiefly that he felt separation was nothing but the first step toward divorce, that I would have to be the one to leave the house, etc. The notion of divorce carries with it so many overwhelming factors that I simply couldn't deal with it. I have for myself time to "feel into" Walter's proposal that we stay together and attempt to be continually conscious and communicative about what was happening between us.

I knew I had to have the separation. So for a while I have been alone in San Francisco, apartment-sitting for a friend. And in my solitude I've been discovering just how much of myself I possess.

This month has been a most amazing time of growth—of feeling stronger, of beginning to trust in my feelings. Having broken out of some of the barriers, I've received confirmation of the rightness and the truth of those feelings.

Having been shaken up by my leaving, Walter decided to go to a Stanley Keleman workshop along with me. It was quite an experience! Stanley picked up the difficulty in my chest instantly—and had me repeat, "I will not be oppressed. I will not be submissive." He asked me at the end if I would be willing to give up the sexual pleasure I now enjoyed in order not to be oppressed. At first I didn't know exactly what he meant, then decided that that in fact was what I had done in separating from Walter! (Stanley knew we were married, but that's all he knew about us.)

When Stanley worked with Walter, he said that he "sensed danger" with Walter, and wondered which button he pressed would produce a rage. Then he told Walter, after questioning him about his vocation and spiritual commitment, that he didn't believe in his spirituality, that he sounded insecure and threatened. Then Stanley had him go into pounding the bed and saying to his parents: *"You took away my body,"* etc.

What I realized was that Walter's whole life was built on his religious pursuits as a compensation, and I had been a threat, all the more as I got into my own body. And he couldn't stand to have that structure threatened. I had to be tightly controlled; the life in me had to be oppressed. (Of course, this fit in all too well with my own neurosis.) I saw with new clarity why I had had to get away. Walter had continued what had begun in my childhood: I was dying—and had to run for my life.

For all the reasons that you know—the dependency, weakness, and all the realistic, practical considerations—made it so difficult for me to get to the point of asserting myself decisively. But Al, I've done it! One step at a time. And I've found I quite literally have to live one day at a time, refusing to *jump ahead to decisions and problems that don't have to be dealt with now. I spend a lot of time working on grounding and breathing.*

Walter has for the first time, I think, begun to realize and face where I am and why. He is open and working on change—and hopes to do more sessions with Stanley Keleman. This is very hopeful. Yet, I'm staying with my own intuitions and feeling responses to him, which as yet are no different. It may be that the old patterns of easy accommodation to one another will prove too great a risk to continued growth and life for each of us. I at least have to be certain that growth and life are not hampered.

So my focus now is myself—and the question of the marriage is one to be answered on another day—farther down the road.

While staying in the apartment in San Francisco, I had learned about an international Bioenergetic conference to be held in Aspen, Colorado in mid-summer. Because I was to begin training in Bioenergetic Analysis when we returned to New York, I was particularly interested in attending the four-day conference where I could learn more about the method, and meet new people who practiced it.

Looking back, it's amazing it worked out that I could leave my children and fly to Aspen. When I arrived at the conference, high in the Rockies, I began to meet other people who were engaged in Bioenergetics—as trainers, students, and clients. As had been the case at Satori the summer before, I found them open, energetic, full of feeling. I was immediately intrigued and inspired by the ambience, the energy. I felt quickly and deeply drawn into this group of people.

Al Lowen gave the opening address, and of course I was proud and inspired to experience my therapist in his role as founder and leader of Bioenergetic Analysis.

The big surprise came later in the day. The afternoon speaker came on stage, dressed in white pants and a baby blue shirt. He sat casually on the edge of a table, and began his lecture entitled, "New Wine in Old Wineskins." With a smile and twinkly eyes he talked about Bioenergetics and character structure using Biblical references. I was astonished! Here was a man with a similar background to mine who was speaking about what was most important to me. And his name was Robert Hilton.

After the presentation, I went up to the speaker and introduced myself. Then I said, "Your speech made me think of *The Ground of Being*, by Paul Tillich. Are you familiar with that?" He smiled and said, "Of course!" I could tell he was a bit impressed.

That night, the conference attendees went to a well-known night club in the center of Aspen. When we entered the band was playing rather softly and nothing was happening. Then, as the conference crowd filled the dance floor, the place came alive.

I saw right away that Bob Hilton was at a nearby table, talking with a colleague. After a time he came over and asked me if I'd like to dance. I was thrilled—and quite surprised at how amazing he was on the dance floor! He had great rhythm, easy flow, easy to follow. It was for me a magical moment. Here was a man who, prior to becoming involved in Bioenergetics and establishing a training institute in Southern California, had been a pastor and a seminary professor. He had had an intense religious background, as had I. And here we were, at a Bioenergetic conference, dancing together!

At the end of the conference I left the hotel to board a small plane for the short flight to Denver. The weather was not good, and the little plane bounced jarringly as it darted through the mountains in the unstable air. At moments it was terrifying, and I wondered if we would make it to our destination. We did, of course. But the bumpy flight was a portent of the journey to come.

A month or so later, my new friend Eleanor Greenlee, whom I had met at a workshop with Earl Cramer, invited me to drive with her to Newport Beach for a meeting and party for people involved in Bioenergetics. I was looking forward to seeing once more those I had met in Aspen. And it was my secret hope to see Bob Hilton again. For the party I brought along a full-length flowery dress with a matching stole, which I called my Scarlet O'Hara dress.

Finally, Bob Hilton arrived—with his date. Both dressed in white. He said hello. But we didn't dance.

It would take ten years.

Inner Journey II

I was enjoying my night course at Columbia School of Social Work. One particular homework assignment, an article by William Schwartz, inspired me deeply:

"... *we may view artistic activity as an attempt, by someone innately endowed with extreme sensitivity to the world about him, to express strong personal feelings and aspirations through a disciplined use of his materials. The analogy between the helping agent [the therapist] and the creative artist can be struck at several points. In both, there is an emphasis on feeling, on an empathic quality which is cherished as a tool of the craft; both feel a constant need for fresh insights into the nature of things and for new ways to express their view of the world; in both, there is the strong preoccupation with essences and basic principles; there is a high degree of subjectivity, of self-consciousness, which constitutes a major element in their ability to create new vistas and new perspectives; in both, the creativity is nourished by the continuous search for truth and is, in fact, an expression of this search; and both require an atmosphere in which one is free to explore, to err, to test reality, and to change."*

In my journal I wrote the following response:

In my own personality and character there is a strong identification with the artist, though skill and talent have not combined in any one area so that I could presume to call myself such. Now, to have the "disciplined uniqueness" of the therapist likened to the artist, I find thrilling!

Some months later I wrote the following:

There are two sides of me which I call the conflict between the Good Lady and the Prodigal Daughter: the polite, proper, cool, conventional lady and the call-it-like-it-is, I'll-do-what-I-please woman.
  Neither of those aspects in me lives too comfortably with the other. And neither abdicates to the other.
  This takes me to the artist in me, that I wrote about earlier. The Prodigal Daughter and the artist are one and the same. The artist wants to say—I move from my feelings—and go where they take me . . . unfettered by convention, because it is only out of freedom that I can see clearly, and reflect truly what I see. And speak. My creative energy

is unbound and flows freely in response to the moment . . . and finds its mark.

But the voice of the artist is so <u>small</u>. And lacks courage. And the other side—the Good Lady—is strong, strengthened by time and necessity and some experiences gone bad. <u>That</u> side says, this is the way it has to be: order, reason, control; acceptance of the Way Things Are, abiding by rules (keep it in, keep it tight). You won't get hurt that way (you only <u>hurt</u>). And you're less likely to hurt anyone else. Avoid the pain, don't cause the pain. (Just accept the pain of your struggle.)

Neither side can abdicate. The artist represents life. For the artist to give up would be death to me. To be sure, the kind of death I see many people living. But I cannot survive with <u>less</u> of the artist in me.

And yet I seem unable to choose very much more. The other side can't abdicate to the artist. Why? Because that means risking <u>everything</u>—or so it seems. Everything—lifestyle, comfort, security—expendable. But family—husband? children?

Those, it appears to me, are the possible choices at the extremes: death on the one hand, and life at the risk of all one has on the other. . . . Most people, I think, really have no choice. The real artist has no choice. She is an artist because she cannot be anything else. And in most others, the artist doesn't exist because it was never allowed to come to life.

But I have a choice. (I sometimes feel I'm <u>cursed</u> with a choice.) And it seems that my life dictates *that I choose both. The artist <u>and</u> the other . . . and live with the discomfort. The struggle for me is to change the balance. The voice of the artist—the "prodigal"—<u>has</u> to become stronger, clearer. Less afraid. And <u>must believe in itself</u>.*

Back to School

After our return to New York in 1972, I immediately began the application process for Columbia School of Social Work. I was fully committed to obtaining the education needed to expand my capacity to become a practicing psychotherapist. I was surprised and thrilled to have the recommendation of the lecturer of the night course I enrolled in:

Mrs. Beitrice Seitzman
Director of Admissions
Dear Mrs. Seitzman:

I am writing to you about Mrs. Virginia Wink, a student in my class. In my opinion, Mrs. Wink is such an exceptional student that upon hearing that she was applying for admission to the School of Social Work I offered to write this letter for her, without her requesting it.

She, first of all, is highly competent intellectually, receiving the highest grade in the mid-term examination—just short of a perfect paper. Prior to the examination, however, I had already formed the impression, albeit on the basis of rather limited experience with her as a student, that was highly positive. On the basis of her classroom participation, I gained the impression that she is a mature woman, intellectually curious, and with a certain quality about her that speaks for very solid relationships with people. I would put her in the class, again impressionistic, of those students whom I would regard as "exceptional." From this vantage point, her application for admission deserves the most serious consideration.

Sincerely yours,
Norton S. Eisenberg, MD
Lecturer, Psychiatric Area

I was all the more thrilled to learn that I had been accepted into the graduate program—*and* received a scholarship grant. (I'm sure that the lecturer's *very* gracious letter must have played a role in both.) In January 1974, I received the following:

Dear Mrs. Wink

As you are aware, the Fellowship Committee awarded you a scholarship grant of $3,180 for the academic year 1973–74.

I think you will be pleased to know that $2,500 of this grant is part of the Mary Antoinette Cannon Fellowship which is awarded annually to students of outstanding potential.

Best wishes this semester.

*Yours sincerely,
Rubina B.
Assistant Director of Admissions
& Financial Aid Officer*

In the fall of 1973 I entered Columbia School of Social Work for the two-year program for the master's degree in Social Work. In addition to a full course load there was the field work for a number of hours a week. The first year I was assigned to a senior retirement home for Jewish residents, the second year to St. Luke's Hospital. (Fortunately, both were nearby.) I very much enjoyed the courses and all that I was learning in the field.

At the same time, I began the training program to become a certified Bioenergetic therapist. This was a four-year course that met mostly on Saturdays, many times a year, and included weekend seminars and week-long conferences. The program also included individual therapy and supervision.

Full-time graduate school and Bioenergetic training on weekends! This had a tremendous impact on family life. When Becca was an adult she said to a friend, "When my mother went back to school when I was seven years old, I had to cook dinner for the family every night!" What?

Well, it wasn't quite like that. The fact is, she was assigned to set the table for dinner and rotated with her brothers on clean-up duty. (A young college student, the daughter of friends who lived near us during our student days, stayed in our so-called servant's room for a while, and cooked our evening meals.) But clearly Becca must have felt abandonment during that time, and, as is so often the case, the sense that responsibility for the family was somehow on her shoulders.

My heavy schedule also impacted the lives of Steve and Chris. As young teenagers they must have felt many times that they, along with their younger sister, did not have the attention, the parental presence and, therefore, the stability they needed and should have received. So why would I undertake such a demanding task—getting a master's degree *and* Bioenergetic training at the same time?

The answer was quite simple. If Walter and I got a divorce, I would have to be able to support myself and my kids.

So, what was happening in the family?

Family Time

Soon after we moved into Knox Hall, we established a "house church," weekly gatherings with good friends: Walter's New Testament colleague, Lou Martyn, and his wife, Dot, and their three sons; and another professor, Jim Bergland, his wife June, and their two sons. We met on Thursday evenings, alternating houses, and engaged with the kids in a simple service. For us all this was pretty much the extent of our church-going (except for special services at Riverside Church, across the street from the seminary, and the Episcopal Cathedral of St. John the Divine, just a few blocks away). The Martyns and the Berglands had country homes where they went on weekends. Soon, so would we.

Jim and June Bergland frequently invited us to their large farm in Blandford, Massachusetts. We loved visiting there and roaming the property and the surrounding countryside. We began looking in the area for homes for sale, and finally we settled on one just down the road, close to the nearest tiny town of Russell. It was a small cabin on

Our cottage in the country

eight acres of forested land, with a stream flowing in front of it. I recall the price was $14,000! For us it was a great weekend get-away. The kids loved being there, cross-country skiing in the winter months, playing in the stream, and wandering in the woods throughout the year.

Along with brief and frequent interactions in the city, we spent fun weekends with the Grovers, the family I met at the time of Chris's birth. Their first born, Cindy, was a child actor on a long-running soap opera. With the money she earned the family bought a vacation home on Candlewood Lake in Connecticut. We enjoyed occasional overnights there with them in the summertime, swimming and waterskiing on the lake, and in the winter, playing in the snow.

After we returned to New York from our years in Hitchcock, I reconnected with my SMU friend, Rebecca Sloan. She and her husband, Malcom Bowers, had divorced. She moved with her three children into a two-story house in a village in the Catskills, where she spent her days painting. She had discovered the artist in her, and she happily embraced the hippy lifestyle that was burgeoning at that time. Rebecca's children, Steve, Robbie, and Andrea, were about the same ages as our kids. Our family loved to spend exciting weekends with them in the Catskills—the children playing adventuresome games, the adults enjoying music, dancing, and exposure to Rebecca's artistic creations. Sadly, after several years there, Rebecca's life fell apart. We lost contact for a period of time, then finally reconnected when she returned to New York.

I always felt very close to Rebecca. I was happy and grateful that Steve and Chris and I were able to attend her seventieth birthday celebration in Montauk, Long Island, with her family and mutual friends. Only a few months later she was diagnosed with cancer. I was able to visit my dearly beloved friend in her New York apartment before she passed away toward the end of the year.

We were joined in the Catskills several times by other friends from SMU days. One such couple was Betty Crump and her husband, Ken Hanson. Betty had gone to New York to pursue her doctorate from Columbia University, and met and married Ken, a British research biochemist at New York University Medical School. They moved to Orange, Connecticut, and Betty became an acclaimed professor at the University of Connecticut. Eventually, Ken devoted full time to his interest in photography. He made numerous hiking trips to the Himalayas with camera equipment on his back. Many of his incredible photographs appear in his breathtaking book, *Himalayan Portfolios*. We loved visiting with Betty and Ken and their two children, Patrick and Gaelen, in the Catskills, and we also had the pleasure of visiting them at their home in Orange and their second home in Coventry. They joined us in our country cottage in Massachusetts, and I am happy to say that I have remained in touch with these very special friends!

One summer, my parents decided to join us for a vacation trip. All seven of us managed to get into our station wagon—with camping gear on the roof—and headed for the Maritime Provinces.

The first stop was a campground on Cape Cod. The adults slept in a regular tent, and the kids in a small pop-up. Pretty doggone crowded! We drove from there to Bar Harbor in Maine, where we got on a ferry to Yarmouth, Nova Scotia. We enjoyed driving through the lovely island, walking on the shores—and sleeping in motels at night!

Our daily outings had landed us in a part of Prince Edward Island where we had to haul out our tents again. Delightful surroundings, but with an enemy. There was an infestation of black flies—something we had never experienced before. We ended up miserably covered with bites. We fled from our campsite as fast as we could in the morning.

By noon we had another first-time experience, one that was not painful at all. Stopping for lunch at a small café on the road, we saw on the menu, sautéed fiddlehead ferns. What? I had never heard of them before—nor have I come across them since. Too bad. They were absolutely scrumptious—and healthy, too, apparently!

Before we left Prince Edward Island, we had a special evening outing to see the *Anne of Green Gables* musical. It was performed outdoors at an arts center in Charlottetown,

Betty and Virginia out for a run

The family in Nova Scotia

the home of the author of the classic children's novel. The children enjoyed viewing this world-famous story on stage, along with a large number of tourists, in the midst of our wanderings.

On the last day we drove down the coast of New Brunswick and began the long drive back to New York City. It had been a delightful trip, made quite special by having the grandparents sharing it with us.

Noni and Papaw

The Kids

Steve

After Steve completed the sixth grade at Agnes Russell, he had to find a new school. We were thrilled that he was accepted into Dalton, perhaps the most elite private school in Manhattan. (Our son was the "token Protestant," we thought.) It was a different world, and Steve had to travel to the East side—89th Street off of Park Avenue—to get to class each day.

Around Steve's thirteenth birthday, we decided to have a party and invite his Dalton friends. We prepared a table full of goodies and looked forward to some fun when the dozen or so guests would arrive at seven p.m. But at about six o'clock the phone started ringing. "I'm sorry, I can't come to your house tonight, Steve . . ." And it kept ringing. Finally, *everyone* had cancelled! Apparently, the parents didn't want their thirteen-year-olds coming to our address on the upper West Side—too close to Harlem. (They may not have known that we were in the Columbia University neighborhood.) But how devastating for our young son!

The family sat around the table and nibbled away at the fancy food we had prepared, trying to think of light-hearted subjects to talk about. Steve shared with us his experience that day while at school. We had given him a Timex watch for his birthday, which he was very excited to receive. But at school, when he proudly showed it to a friend, the boy just looked away. Not a cool watch—too cheap!

Five years later, Steve would have a very different birthday experience. On May 1, 1976, he was turning eighteen, a few weeks before his high school graduation. We planned a surprise party for him, and almost the entire senior class showed up! They loved our home. We were living in Knox Hall, and our apartment was probably more expansive than many of the wealthy East Siders' living quarters. The kids had a blast. They danced, sang— and some couples quietly went upstairs to one of the bedrooms that became the go-to place to "make out."

When it was over long after midnight and the mob of high school seniors went home, Walter and I were enormously relieved and extremely grateful that the earlier experience of disappointment and shame had been beautifully vindicated. He was acknowledged and honored by his friends and fellow classmates the way we—as parents, of course—felt certain he deserved.

Steve enjoyed his years at Dalton and has maintained relationships with many of his school friends. A particularly close friend was Michael Rogosin, who lived on the West Side with his father, Lionel, a prize-winning documentary filmmaker.

During the junior high years Steve played football and soccer, and later joined the wrestling team. That ended when he had a concussion—scary, but fortunately, not too serious. During after-school hours he focused more and more on his music.

He also took a jewelry-making class during his junior year. He designed and made a necklace that he presented to me. This pendant would forever remain my favorite piece of jewelry. I was so grateful that Steve's creativity manifested itself in the necklace I loved—and would wear constantly from the day I received it.

For Steve's first years in high school we did not establish a curfew. (I don't remember why not!) Therefore, he pretty much did what he wanted with a very busy social life after hours. But we became well aware that his grades were going down—not what we expected from Steve. We then put in place a strict schedule, and the grades went back up. We were not aware that he had acquired a regular habit of smoking pot, beginning in 1972 during our stay in Berkeley. (This continued until 1979, when Steve became allergic to cannabis, with symptoms of heart palpitations. That ended the pot smoking for good!)

In 1975, at the end of his junior year, Steve, along with his friends, Michael Rogosin and David Martyn, decided to take a coming-of-age journey. As soon as he turned seventeen on the first of May, Steve acquired his driver's license, and the other two boys got theirs soon after. These novice drivers were going to set out across the country, all the way to California. The parents were anxious about this adventure but had been convinced by the kids to give it a "go." We said, "Yes," but held our breath for the next few weeks.

Michael, who had access to plenty of money, provided a large motor home, which was filled with steaks and food of all sorts. The three musketeers excitedly packed up their clothes and found their seats in the unfamiliar vehicle, with Steve as the senior driver. (After all, he'd had his license for a full three weeks!) They headed West, and finally ended up in Los Angeles. (We learned eventually that they had visited a massage parlor there. Well, it's coming-of-age time, right?) And they were guests in the Malibu vacation home of one of their classmates. Then they headed north to Big Sur.

When these inexperienced drivers reached Highway One, they found the winding coastal road to be overwhelming. They passed many hitchhikers along the way, and one of the boys said, "Hey, let's pick up one of those guys and he can drive us." "Good idea!" Well, not really.

The boys pulled off to the side of the road and opened the door for a sunburned hiker with a long ponytail, eager for the ride. They soon realized their new driver was quite high on something. The motor home lurched forward as he slammed the gas pedal to the floor. He hummed tunes while he made the sharp turns so fast the large vehicle rounded on two wheels! The boys rolled onto the floor from one side to the other. "He's gonna kill us!" Steve shrieked. They yelled at the guy to stop, then they told him to get out. And fortunately, he did.

The wanderers made it to Big Sur on their own, and thoroughly enjoyed the rest of their trip without any mishaps. Their parents were enormously relieved when Steve, David, and Michael returned home safely.

All through Steve's life as a teenager, he loved his classes at school, his girlfriends, his guy buddies. And a most significant thing in his life was his music: playing the guitar

Steve, Rebecca, and guitar

and singing. Before we left Hitchcock, we bought him a guitar and he had his first lessons there. As time went by, he began to sing as he played, as well as to compose songs of his own, and then to perform. This talent and interest would continue to be expressed throughout Steve's very active and successful life.

During Steve's senior year he said to us one day, "Mom, Dad, I've decided I'm not going to college." What? How could that be?

"I want to continue studying guitar, writing songs, and singing and recording. That's my interest. That's what I'm going to do," Steve informed us. Walter and I were stunned. We did not expect this. We were proud of his musical talent and wanted him to continue developing it, but *instead* of college? He was clear and determined. So, in fairly short order we agreed to support him in his decision. (Dalton was probably shocked as well. The percentage rate of their graduates who went to college was very likely near 100%. Steve Wink was going to mess with that? Well, he would more than make up for it.)

It's too bad that I can't include here a recording of Steve playing his guitar and singing a song he wrote. But since that's not possible, here are the lyrics to one of his many songs:

Wittgenstein's Ladder
It has taken, taken me this long
To get beyond belief
I climb up your ladder
I throw it back down
How will it feel, if I hit the ground
It isn't nothing, no it isn't nothing
It's always something, beyond belief

I'm taking your lesson
What did I learn
You're quick to judgment
And I'm a slow burn
How will I know you
If you change your ways
If nothing still looks like
It looks like today

It isn't nothing, no it isn't nothing
It's always something, beyond belief

It's got to be real, it's got to be true
So far from hopeless, it's got to be you

Chris

It's interesting how certain proclivities in childhood—even unacceptable ones—get expressed quite creatively in adult life. From a very early age Chris liked to push the boundaries, go farther, do surprising things. While we were living in Knox Hall, one thing he loved to do at dinnertime was to throw a piece of spaghetti up in the air and catch it in his mouth as it fell toward the table. The only ones he didn't catch were several strands that were thrown so hard they stuck to the very high ceiling (and remained hanging there for a long time). He also had his little sister throw grapes at him from across the room, moving quickly so they always landed in his mouth. This activity, for which he was sometimes admonished, showed up in a different—and very popular—form a number of years later!

After entering Agnes Russell School, Chris dashed off to class each morning, going through the seminary and across Broadway to Columbia Teacher's College. Once he dragged with him a heavy piece of exercise equipment he had gotten for Christmas, so he could show it to his new classmates. And then there was another time. . . .

I received a phone call from the front entrance of the seminary: "Mrs. Wink, your son is involved in an accident. You should come immediately. He's across the street!" I raced out of the apartment in a panic, ran the shortest route through the tunnel to the seminary, and out the entry door at 120th and Broadway. I could see my little boy across the street, sitting on the curb with a policeman standing over him and a parked taxicab nearby. It was miserable waiting for the light to change before rushing to him and holding him tight.

"Chris, are you okay? What happened?" I squealed, breathless.

The policeman soberly told me that as Chris had run across 120th St., the cab driver made a right turn onto Broadway, slamming on his breaks when he finally caught sight of the boy, but knocked him over. He was frightened, but no apparent injuries. This was confirmed after a visit to the ER at St. Luke's hospital, mandated by the police. What a disaster that could have been! Chris had avoided another unthinkable tragedy, way worse than losing an eye because of a BB shot. We were eternally grateful. And, *we all* became more conscious and careful when crossing streets in New York City!

While we were in California on sabbatical, Chris turned eleven years old. That meant it was his turn for the "grandmother trip." He told Noni he wanted to go to Hawaii, and she was all for it. Noni landed in San Francisco where Chris joined her, and they flew to Honolulu. They were there for several days, visiting Pearl Harbor and other significant places, and taking a ride in a glass-bottomed boat. Chris, on his own, rented a surfboard and learned how to use it. Then the two of them went to the Big Island to visit the volcanoes. In the couple of years prior, Chris had acquired a great interest in geology. He began to gather what became an enormous collection of rocks: geodes and other stones of different shapes and sizes. The Big Island was certainly the place to go to see more and learn more about his new hobby. He and Noni had a great time.

A year or so after we returned from California, a seminary student told Chris about his adventurous experiences at a summer camp in the Southwest. It sounded like just what this young teenager would want to do next. He enrolled for the Prairie Trek Expedition, sponsored by the Cottonwood Gulch Foundation in New Mexico, and headed off for what would be a truly amazing experience. We were blown away by the letter we received from him.

Dear family,

We left this morning on our last overnight of the summer, climbing Miller Peak in the Huachuca Mountains in Arizona (five miles from the Mexican border). On the way up I was thinking of all the things I had learned this summer. I felt I had grown a lot. I hiked ahead and was all alone at one point. I turned on the radio and "Morning Has Broken" was on. At that moment I had just gotten to the top of a ridge and could see forever! Suddenly I noticed the heavenly smell of all the wildflowers around me, and the sounds of the birds. "Morning has broken, like the first morning!! Blackbird has spoken, like the first bird!" I started to dance as I walked, singing and looking as I went. Picking up the wildflowers, smelling them and throwing them into the air. I followed them and dived in the air also. Then I reached into my back pocket and took out my aggressions and burned them under a rock and walked away from it. I felt lighter! "Praise for the singing, praise for the morning!! Still dancing I went further looking at my world and I felt like I was really a part of it. Then, the sun grew bright, the flowers started glowing and the birds chirped louder! Chills went down my back and I saw my joy flying in the air and jumped up to kiss it. I did a summersault in the air, grabbed it and came down and realized that I had landed in a new body and had left my old one on the trail. My new one was filled with vitality and glowed like the stars. I liked it. After walking further, I looked back at my old self lying on the trail. I felt sad to leave it, but happy once I looked straight up the trail. Morning for me had just broken. I felt glad that I was alive and I screamed loudly in pure joy, hearing it echo off the mountains. I walked faster on my trail, and as I did the flowers waved the leaves in front of me. Hosanna! Then I was on top of my mountain and I could see all around. Then all of the energy from everywhere I could see came out of the ground and jumped into me! I felt borderless. Then I realized that my trail continued down into the valley and over the next peak, and the next and the next. I was only at the beginning of my trail, and this was the first morning of my hike. The trail went into the horizon and I could not see the end.

Love,
Chris

How's that . . . for a fourteen-year-old?

As indicated in his letter, Chris loved to run. In high school he joined the track team and won his very first race. I don't remember Chris ever *not* winning. At another meet he won a 440 and an 880 back to back, making a record which still stands at Fieldston School. There was a price to pay: Chris woke up the next day with his back muscles so constricted that he was unable to move and was in painful agony. I took him to an acupuncturist who thankfully brought him back to normal.

Track wasn't the only sport Chris excelled in. He was great at football. He could catch any pass that was thrown. I was on hand to watch an unbelievable catch that won the game. At another game I was standing on the side of the field when he came running with the ball, and an opposing team member pushed him roughly out of bounds and down to the ground, a few feet away from me. I started screaming at the boy, "What are you doing to him? Stop that!" (Did I embarrass my son? Maybe. I never heard.)

Chris paid close attention to keeping in shape, following the rules and expectations of his coaches. He watched his diet, avoided alcohol and pot, and kept up regular exercise. In fact, there were times he actually jogged all the way to school—from our home in Manhattan to Fieldston in Riverdale (the Bronx).

Soon after we moved back to New York we gave Chris a drum set for Christmas. He loved shaking the walls of the apartment with his drumbeats. Certain restrictions had to be set in order to protect neighbors on all sides, but he kept learning and playing; as it turned out, drums would play a very central role in Chris's future. (Sorry there's no available photo!)

Chris continued enthusiastically with his drum lessons and his love of music. Once I attended an event held in the basketball gym of his school. I don't remember the details, but I vividly recall Chris, rhythmically beating a snare drum. Gradually, he increased the volume and the speed and the intensity until the entire gym was in a joyful uproar! (Another preview of things to come!)

Toward the end of his junior year of high school, Chris began to talk with us about an adventure he wanted to take in the summer.

"My buddy, Bobby, and I had a great idea the other day. We want to go on a long bike ride somewhere fun. We thought about taking a train down to Florida, and then riding bikes all the way down to the end of the state. Wouldn't that be cool?"

Cool? How about *scary*. Of course not! was our initial reaction. But Chris kept it up, and finally he convinced us to agree to the plans. In midsummer the two boys loaded their bikes on the train that took them to Jacksonville, Florida. With much excitement they disembarked and began their very long bike ride.

The boys rode along the coast to Daytona, then turned inland in the direction of Orlando, and soon came into swampy terrain. Each night they stopped at a campground and set up the plastic tube to sleep in. There were crocodiles moving about in nearby water, but it was tiny critters that caused the big problem. One night at Flintstone Campground Bobby was inundated with black flies. He had painful bites all over his skin and was miserable. The boys had to find a doctor so that he could be treated. They found a hotel to sleep in for a night, and, fortunately, Bobby was pain free after a couple of days.

They got on their bikes to head for Disney World, but they were stopped by police, who said bikes weren't allowed. There were no bike paths on the road. But the officers were considerate, and actually escorted them there. After a fun day at the park, checking out all the rides, they returned by bus to the campground, and the next day mounted their bikes for Miami.

The boys spent a couple of nights at the home of friends of friends, while checking out the city and surrounding areas. Then back to the campgrounds. Finally, after almost two weeks of adventure on their own, Chris and Bobby boarded the train and headed for home. Weary and satisfied, they knew that they had indeed *come of age*!

Rebecca

When she was seven years old, Rebecca began taking ballet lessons at the School of American Ballet at Lincoln Center. She loved it and was thrilled to be chosen by New York City Ballet to be in their production of *The Nutcracker Suite*. For two seasons she performed on stage as an angel and a soldier. Many years later, Becca would teach creative dance classes for inner-city children at California Dance Institute in Los Angeles, a subsidiary of the National Dance Institute founded by Jacques D'Amboise—who played the prince during the two seasons that Becca was in the NYC Ballet. (Again, no picture. So sad!)

When the family returned from the Sabbatical in California Becca started school at Agnes Russell, as her brothers had done some years earlier. She liked her first-grade teacher, Jill, but by the time she started second grade the school was falling apart and most of the teachers were gone. Agnes Russell shut down at the end of the year.

Becca moved to Ethical Culture School, and she discovered that being accepted as a new student in third grade was not easy. On her first day of school I sent her off in a flouncy dress and shiny shoes—not okay! She came home hurt and unhappy, saying that she had been mocked. The other students were wearing jeans. And after another school day she hung her head and said:

"A girl named Carrie made fun of me today because I don't know any sports. She doesn't understand there was no place to play sports at Agnes Russell!"

Why are kids so hard on each other? Things did get better fairly soon. Eventually, even Carrie became one of her many good friends.

In thinking back over Becca's life, a theme that comes to mind is *travel*. She really had an amazing amount of it, beginning at a very young age—a number of far-flung adventures, fun and exciting times near and far, and a couple of harrowing experiences while "on the road."

Our daughter loved the visits with her grandparents in the summer (as did her brothers), especially when staying at their house on the beach. They loved playing in the sand, wading in the warm Gulf water, swinging in the hammock—everything to do in that—for them—magical place.

There were many family trips to Texas to see the grandparents. Then, in the summer when she was eight years old, Becca wanted so badly to spend time on the beach with Noni and PaPaw. Her brothers were in summer camp, and I was in graduate school. There was no family trip planned. "Can I please go by myself to Texas?" she pleaded. After a time, we agreed. (*An eight-year-old—can you believe it?*)

We got Becca seated on the plane, and the stewardess—so-called in those days—assured us she would be carefully looked after during the three-hour flight. When the plane landed in Houston, she was escorted into the airport. Becca expected to see her beloved grandparents waving to her. But . . . there was no one there to meet her! (How fortunate we are these days to have cell phones.) The stewardess asked Becca for her grandmother's name so that she could page her over the intercom. Becca only knew her as "Noni."

"Do you know her first name?" the stewardess asked. Tentatively, Becca replied, "I think it might be Ethel." (Her name was actually Hazel.) Finally, after about half an hour (during which time the airport was paging one "Ethel Conerly," over and over), my parents came running into the airport where Becca was tightly clutching the hand of the patient flight attendant. (A half hour is a *very* long time to wait when you are all alone—and don't know why.) The grandparents hugged and hugged Rebecca, and explained to a relieved flight attendant how they had been caught in a traffic jam, some kind of accident on the highway, and, when at last cars could move, they had sped to the airport as fast as they were able.

"You're a brave little girl!" the flight attendant told Becca as they said goodbye.

When she was fifteen, Rebecca took another trip alone—this time to Paris. I had gone to France the year before to teach a training group in the home of one of the trainees. I enjoyed the people in the group, working with them, and being in the elegant home in the outskirts of Paris. The owner and I discovered we had daughters about the same age. She urged me to send Becca over for a vacation with them in the summertime. Becca loved that idea, so we began to plan her adventure.

I was happy and anxious about putting my daughter on the overnight flight to Paris. She was almost twice the age she'd been when she flew by herself to Houston. But now she was flying alone over the Atlantic to another country! Her excitement exceeded her anxiety. She gave me a tight hug and waved goodbye as she walked toward the plane. I went back to my apartment and slept on and off during the night, eager to get the "I have arrived!" call. It came, and she assured me she had been warmly welcomed by the host family, who certainly arrived at Charles de Gaulle airport on time.

Then, less than an hour later there was another call—a frantic one.

"Mom!" she cried. "I'm at their house. I'm *dying* to pee! I went to the bathroom, but the toilet doesn't have a seat! What can I do?

Fortunately, I remembered the house well.

"That's a *bidet*, not a toilet," I said. "Go out the door, turn left, and walk to the end of the hall. The toilet is there."

With enormous relief she said, "Thanks, Mom," and abruptly hung up the phone. I understood the instant departure.

Becca had an amazing vacation, taking the metro into the city and visiting all the main attractions, traveling along the Seine to small villages, enjoying French cuisine. And, as had I on my first and later trips to Paris, she learned a lot about the differences in our cultures (including the way bathrooms were outfitted!).

In the summer of 1975 when Becca was nine years old, the family flew to Virgin Gorda in the British Virgin Islands. A New York couple we knew owned a house on a hillside there, and offered it to us for a week's stay. Becca and her brothers (and parents) had a marvelous time exploring the island and snorkeling in the pristine waters inhabited by fascinating sea-life.

In the summer of '77 it was Becca's turn to have her special eleven-year-old vacation trip with Noni. Becca chose Japan (she wanted to travel as far away as possible, and at the time, China was not open for travel by Americans), and I was invited to go along. We flew from New York to San Francisco (where Becca would live a decade later), and then to Tokyo. I still recall summoning my energy after we landed, trying to stay alert, squeezing my daughter's hand as we slowly moved with an unbelievable mass of people into the immigration terminal.

Noni's travels were always carefully planned, comfortable, and safe. We were met with a white-gloved driver who took us to our hotel in the Ginza district. We saw the sights of the city, moved on to the lovely experience of staying in a *ryokan* (traditional Japanese inn) in Kyoto, took the highspeed train to view Fujiyama, and felt the spiritual overwhelm of the Buddhist temple in Nara.

I fell in love with the aesthetic of Japan. Forever after I would be drawn to the architecture and the art, the gardens, and for that matter, the food. It all felt soothing to my soul. I bought a screen in Kyoto, as well as a couple of prints, and these articles would influence the interior decorating of my living spaces in the years thereafter.

My mother, my daughter, and I were sad to leave Japan. On our way home we enjoyed a couple of days in Hong Kong, viewing the city, cruising the harbor in a small boat, enjoying a Chinese barbecue on Victoria Peak, and taking the tram down to the city.

We also had a stop in Honolulu, staying, as always when traveling with Noni, at a fine hotel. Becca was particularly excited by the famous luau we attended on the shore.

Becca was an enthusiastic traveler, eager to learn about Asian cultures. She loved sleeping on the futon in the *ryokan*, and sitting on the floor as the lovely ladies in kimonos conducted a tea ceremony and then prepared our meal. During all the travels this beautiful child, very near the major shift of body and mind into teen years, was unaware of the decision kept secret from her, that would bring about cataclysmic change in her family and impact her life forever. These happy, exciting days in Asia preceded by a month or so the revelation that would bring heartbreak: Her parents were getting divorced.

A Seismic Shift

In January of 1976 my dear grandmother, Clara Belle Moore, passed away at age eighty-nine. I went to Alvin, Texas for the funeral, and reconnected with many Moore family relatives. It was a poignant time of remembering the life of my beloved "Mam-ma," and my many experiences with her (including the time I came to visit her in an apartment when she was in her early eighties, and she insisted on carrying my suitcase up the stairs!). She meant so much to me. I always knew that, for her, my best *was* good enough.

I returned to New York after that sad, yet deeply meaningful time in Texas, only to discover that the problems and tensions in my marriage had intensified to the point of no return. I made it clear that my position was: It's over. We agreed to tell the boys only, and not to make it public until the summer. But we were "separated," and for the time being, living in the same house.

Shortly after that the Union Seminary faculty voted to deny Walter tenure (a decision the seminary eventually regretted). A seismic shift, indeed!

During the Spring of '77 the boys were intensely engaged in their teenaged activities—Steve winding up his high school years, preparing for his performing career, Chris working hard at sports. Both were no doubt continually conscious of the "seismic change" in the family, wondering what was ahead. When we had first told them about the status of our marriage, Chris cried, and Steve maintained a somber expression. As time went by, both seemed to deal with the situation fairly well.

Because we had chosen not to tell her, we assumed Becca was clueless. However, she certainly sensed something was different. In the summertime she went away to summer camp. While there, Walter, without my knowledge, sent a letter to her, telling her that we were separated. I got a concerned call from the camp leader, saying that Rebecca was completely distraught and unable to take part in activities. I was furious. How could he have done this! (I found out much later that he had misunderstood something I said, assuming I *had* informed her.) I drove to her camp to try, as best I could, to console her and assure her that both her parents loved her more than ever.

Eventually, Becca had to adjust to the fact that June, who had been her beloved kindergarten teacher, had become her stepmother. A tough change. And Walter was given credit for everything good, while I was assigned the blame. (Understandable, from a psychological point of view, for her to blame her mother, but so difficult for me, to put it mildly.)

Below is the letter I finally sent to my parents about the end of my marriage:

Sept. 3, 1977

My beloved Mom and Dad,

This letter bears heavy, sad news. I know you have been aware that I've called you almost not at all this summer. And the reason is I've had a heavy heart—and it was not the time to share with you. So I seemed to have had to avoid the contact that would be not quite real and honest. Maybe on some level you were aware of that too.

In fact, I know, Mother, that since the Japan trip (our most beautiful, wonderful, unforgettable dream trip) you have sensed from me that something was not going well. The truth I must tell you now is that Walter and I are separating. I know how hard those words hit you, and you have no idea how I would want to protect you (and my children) from the heartache, the dismay, and the bewilderment that this news must bring you.

But it is a reality that must be accepted and lived with.

Walter and I have been involved during the past half-dozen years with an intense effort at growing and learning and expanding. And at facing as honestly as we could our own inner selves—our "dark" sides along with our strengths and potential. And facing and working at the deficits in the relationship as well. Growing and changing does not lead inevitably toward separating. But with us, at this point it is where we have arrived.

I know that you, like everyone else, will have an overriding need to understand "why." We both feel strongly and absolutely that no good purpose can be served by attempting to explain the "why." We ask you to accept that. We take mutual and equal responsibility for the decision and all that led to it.

We have, of course, experienced a lot of pain and undoubtedly there will be a lot more. The paramount concern in the present is the children—and most particularly, Rebecca. The boys have known about our status since soon after we arrived there (which was, incidentally, just after I returned from Mam-ma's funeral.) Becca was told in the summer. She has said that she knew on the Japan trip that something was wrong. I had thought I would talk to you about the situation while in Hawaii, Mom, but I couldn't bear to spoil for you the trip you had given us.

Becca is talking a lot about her feelings, crying a good bit, but <u>dealing</u> with it, not denying it or holding it in. And for that we are grateful. The boys are beautifully concerned about her, and I think are being very understanding, and handling their own feelings well. Their initial response, as will be yours, was that "Such a thing would never happen to us." But they are, and will be, accepting the fact that indeed and sadly, it has happened to us.

Walter is moving into an apartment on 106th St. And Steve, by the way, has moved into his own apartment at 40 W. 89th St. I will be practicing at home except for one day at the downtown office.

I know that you both love Walter as much as your own (and he said recently that he has felt closer to you than his own parents). I don't want anything to change that. In a recent talk we shared with a lot of love all the things we had gotten from each other: our three marvelous children, twenty-one years that have been far better than most people ever know. Walter says his growth has come from me. And he has given me the support and encouragement that has made it possible for me to get a master's degree and to begin my life's (second) work. We have so much to be thankful for—and are.

Now, about me. You mustn't worry about me. Blessedly I am equipped to make a living. And if we manage well, and I can be wise about not wearing myself out, we can make it fine. There may be times when I need to call up and just be sad, and you can be sad with me, and we can all know that sun shines after a gentle rain.

One thing I ask: Becca occasionally pleads with me to "try harder" or to do something else to make things okay. Of course we have tried, and we have done what could be done. Please pray and picture us each happy. Putting us together in the picture, as someone has said, may be controlling, and not what is best, regardless of our earthly wisdom to the contrary. I know that is hard for you. But I need you, Mom and Dad, to believe in me.

I love you both so very, very much. And I am eternally, everlastingly grateful to have been born to you. I'm sorry for the pain this is for you. But you must know also that inside me, with the pain there is also joy, and peace, and strength.

*Your daughter,
Virginia*

While Walter and I were both still living in Knox Hall, Walter's mentor, Elizabeth Howes, had been invited to give a lecture at Union Seminary. She came to our apartment for a visit afterward. The subject of our separation was on her mind, as well as ours. "Why did you come to this conclusion?" she queried. Walter's response was, "Virginia doesn't love me completely." Dr. Howe's response was, "Only God loves completely."

My slightly shocked, internal response was, "What do you mean I didn't love you completely?!" It took me a long while to realize that, yes, he was right. I didn't love him completely. The wounds I had received early in the marriage and before had shut down parts of me. The shutdown was an effort to protect myself from unbearable hurt and shame. For Walter, the behavior that wounded me, I understood many years later, was *his* way of protecting himself. We each had needs the other couldn't—or wouldn't—meet, needs that had existed long before we met and were created by our early childhood experiences. His need was to have someone to love him completely, to "fill in the cracks" so that he could fulfill his lofty goals in life. Mine was to have a *feelingful* relationship, and to be an equal partner in it. In spite of many similarities, our individual histories and our current interests were taking us in different directions.

On February 3, 1978, Walter delivered the divorce decree. On February 10 he and June Bergland were married at Riverside Church. The three children attended the wedding. It was a difficult day for me. I was in my apartment, feeling my aloneness, wondering what kind of future was ahead for me. Numerous friends called, left messages, understood that it was a tough time. I was able to express my mixed emotions, my relief, my anxiety, and my sorrow—to an extent.

Ten years later: a massage therapist came to our home for our weekly treatment. As I relaxed on the table I suddenly began to cry. I didn't know why at first, but it continued . . . and continued. Why am I crying when I am happily married to the right man for me? At some point it became clear: *I was grieving the loss of the intact family.* The crying went on for the entire hour. Thankfully, the masseuse didn't freak out, didn't question, just stood by attentively. At the end of the session when I looked in the mirror, I discovered that my tongue was black! I'd never before nor since seen anything like that. It was the color of grief—grief that had been held in, not fully expressed and released—until then. Fortunately, my husband understood completely, was in no way threatened, and was grateful along with me that the blackness was no longer in my body.

After several decades of intense teaching, writing, and traveling, Walter was diagnosed with Lewy Body Dementia. He passed away on May 10, 2012. A number of years later, I would write the following letter, while reflecting on my life:

November 22, 2020

To Walter:

For years I longed for completion between us. It never happened. But I intend for this very moment to be completion, in the only way that it can happen.

First of all, I want to say to you that I am deeply grateful for the years we had together. Most particularly for our three incredible children, Steve, Chris, and Rebecca. (We could not have achieved that with anyone else!) The many wonderful experiences we had together as a family—their births, their growing-up years, our travels. Thank you from the bottom of my heart.

I am so sorry that I could not meet your needs, that I did not, could not love you completely. Our individual needs and wants, based on early history, were very different. And neither of us was the person to meet the other's needs. But thankfully we each found that other person. I'm so glad for you that you had June for those many years. Glad she blended so beautifully with you in your teaching approach, and that she was there for you in many ways.

I'm also sorry that I was unable to fully express my anger, frustration etc., along the way. It might have helped to change things. But I guess we both did the best we could in those times. I'm glad you received the acknowledgement and praise for your teaching and your writing that you truly deserved.

And I so hope those last years of your life were filled with love, satisfaction, and peace. I am so grateful to be able to say to you that those words certainly describe my own experience. We found our ways.

With love, from my heart—
Virginia

A week after Walter and June were married, I took the kids on a trip to Puerto Rico. After what we'd all been through, I decided it was time for a vacation. Because of a snowstorm our flight was delayed for hours. We arrived in San Juan at six in the morning (instead of the night before). Steve and I went to check for our rental car, leaving our return tickets with Chris at baggage claim where he was lugging our suitcases off the carousel. When we returned I asked him, "Chris, where are the tickets?" He looked puzzled, then stunned. They had disappeared! He had no idea where or why. Steve and I went back to the airline desk to report the loss. Finally we were able to get into our rental car and head out into early morning rush-hour traffic, feeling anxiety, frustration, and exhaustion.

We drove through the crowded city of San Juan, and finally into the countryside, taking the road toward our destination: Boqueron Beach on the south side of the island. Suddenly, over the crest of a mountain we saw a gorgeous double rainbow—the sign of hope! We began to sing and relax as we drove along. "Well, that says it!" I shouted to the kids. "We're going to have a great time, the four of us!"

And we did. We arrived at the state park and checked

into our cabana, the loveliest one on the beach. We met lots of nice people—many from New York—and one couple turned over to us their hammock and a beach chair when they left the next day. We had lots of fun swimming and playing on the beach, and taking daytime and nighttime excursions. The kids, my dear children, were very sweet to each other and to me. At the end of the week we felt a lot of satisfaction as we packed up to go back home. When we arrived at the airport, we were extremely relieved to find that the stolen tickets had not been used!

* * *

Back in the city we knew, of course, that we had to leave our elegant quarters in Knox Hall. Where would we live? I began looking around and considering options. I finally found what seemed to be just the right apartment at 575 West End Avenue. It was in a lovely building at the corner of 88th St., and the apartment was on the eleventh floor. It had a large living room, a dining room (which became my office), two bedrooms, and a small servant's room behind the kitchen.

Rent was $750 a month. (In the early 2000's, while visiting Steve's apartment on Riverside Drive, I walked the few blocks down to 575 West End Avenue. I told the concierge, seated at his desk inside the entrance, that I'd moved there in 1977 and what I paid for rent. A smile appeared on his face, and after a moment he said, "Do you know how much the rent is today? $10,000 per month!" I was astonished, to put it mildly.)

We had considerably less space in our new environment, but it was more than adequate for our needs, and very pleasant. There was room for my grand piano in the living room, and off to one side, the dining table and chairs. I had the master bedroom, Becca the smaller one, and Chris was fine to sleep in the bunk bed behind the kitchen. I saw my clients in the dining room, which was closed off by French doors and ample enough for my therapy group meetings as well.

I felt freed up by having left the seminary environment. For the kids it was a much more difficult change. They liked the apartment, the building, and the neighborhood, but it was all new and very different. For Chris, it meant that he had farther to go to get to school in Riverdale, but he adjusted. (Distances were never a problem for Chris!) Becca had the hardest time of all. It was tough for her to leave "the best apartment in the whole city." And staying with her father and stepmother on weekends and while I was away became increasingly fraught with ambivalence.

Steve was enormously helpful with the move, and was always quick to respond to needs that showed up within our living space. I commented that he had become "the head of the household": great for me, but undoubtedly a responsibility that would weigh heavily on his young shoulders.

One of the tasks he undertook was to drive me to JFK airport when I was flying off to teach—and to meet me there on my return. What a joy that was for me!

My New Vocation

During my second year at Columbia School of Social Work (and my second year of training in Bioenergetic Analysis) I began to accept clients for psychotherapy. Steve moved into the "servant's quarters" downstairs, and I used his former room upstairs for my office.

After a time, as the number of clients increased, I began to inquire about office space for my practice. A man who was a member of my Bioenergetic training group—I will call him Arthur—offered and encouraged me to take the extra room in his office, which was not too far from my home. It was convenient and inexpensive, so I began practicing there.

In the summer of 1975 Arthur had signed up to lead a retreat at Esalen Institute in Big Sur, and he invited me to assist him. I was happy to have this opportunity. And I was mesmerized by Esalen—the gorgeous location, the atmosphere, the openness.

Arthur, however, was a growing problem. He was handsome and charismatic, and quite a showman. Female attendees were very attracted to him. I became aware that he would disappear with one of them briefly for an intimate encounter, and then reappear as if it were part of the routine. I was shocked and disturbed by this behavior, even though sex between teachers or trainers and students was rather widespread during that time. And, back in the office, when I accidentally discovered that he was having sex with one of his clients, I instantly knew I'd had enough. I told him I was leaving his office. And I did. Immediately. Fortunately, I found that Al Lowen had available space to rent in his headquarters on the East Side.

Sexuality was a major focus in Bioenergetics. Lowen spelled this out in his book, *Love and Orgasm*. In spite of the emphasis on the body and sexuality in Bioenergetics, Lowen, thankfully, did not cross boundaries with patients. During this period there were far more transgressions by therapists from Freudian and Jungian backgrounds who did not deal directly with the body. This subject was a deep concern of mine, and I eventually chaired a committee that presented to the faculty a code of ethics to adopt which made clear the boundaries between therapists and clients. And my doctoral thesis became, "Sexuality in the Therapeutic Process."

During the last year of my Bioenergetic training I was invited to participate at a conference in the Poconos, with people attending from Europe and South America. I had the privilege of leading one of the training groups, utilizing Bioenergetic techniques to deal with the personal issues the participants presented.

This was a thrill and an honor for me. When it was over I was asked by one of the attendees, Mario from Ecuador, if

I would come to Quito and do a week-long workshop. And later, I was contacted by another attendee, Beate from Germany, who urged me to start a training group in Stuttgart. My teaching career had begun!

* * *

I was anxious and excited as I boarded the plane for Ecuador—the first of many trips to cross oceans alone to teach Bioenergetics. Mario met me at the airport and drove me to his home. He and his wife, Maria Luisa, lived in an elegant house outside the city, its rooms filled with paintings, art objects, and what they referred to as archeology—native art created centuries before.

On the morning after my arrival, Mario arranged for their driver to take me into the city on a sightseeing trip. From my comfortable seat in the back of their limo, I could relax and enjoy the view of the beautiful countryside. And then, as we drove along, I began to notice the shacks and hovels by the roadside, and the shabbily dressed adults and children who walked in and out of them. We drove into the center of town and the driver parked the car near the Zocalo in front of the cathedral. I walked slowly through the square, feeling increasingly stricken as I passed blind beggars, people in rags who had lost a limb, mothers holding crying babies, their hands outstretched, hoping to receive a peso or two. I finally reached the entrance to the cathedral, went inside, and sat in a pew. Behind the altar was an enormous statue of Christ with a golden crown of thorns, and large ruby "drops of blood" attached to the side of his cheeks.

I broke into tears and sobbed for minutes. I had come in contact with poverty throughout my life. But what I had experienced since arriving in Ecuador, and that morning on the way to the cathedral, were my first visual encounters with *abject* poverty, and such extreme disparity between rich and poor. As I sat alone in the huge dark space of the cathedral, the overwhelming display of gold and jewels *inside* and the overwhelming poverty and sickness *outside* was literally more than I could bear.

Overall, my trip was a very positive one. I loved working with the Ecuadorean people, and they responded enthusiastically to the Bioenergetic techniques and exercise. They invited me to return the following year. After the workshop Mario and Maria Luisa took me with them to a small village on the shore for a couple of delightful days of rest and relaxation. I felt so grateful for the exposure to the Ecuadorean culture, and for having a beginning understanding of what life for them was like. I returned home with such pleasant memories—and all the tourist items my suitcase could hold.

* * *

Following my trip to Ecuador, and the completion of my Bioenergetic training, I was voted into the faculty. There were very few women trainers at the time, and I was thrilled to help fill that space. And as training groups were established in countries in Europe and South America, there was interest in having a female trainer along with the men. My life would become quite busy with teaching and travel.

I felt that amazing combination of excitement, anticipation, and trepidation as I said goodbye to my three teenaged children, promising we would go out for sushi on my return. Then, after the ride to JFK, I boarded the plane for Stuttgart, Germany.

As I disembarked after the all-night flight, I was relieved to see the familiar face of Beate, and grateful that she had invited me, a neophyte faculty member, to teach the newly formed training group in Stuttgart.

Beate took me to the psychiatric hospital where some members of the group—two psychiatrists, a psychologist, and several social workers—were employed. She led me to a narrow stairway, and as we walked down hundreds of steps between sterile white walls I began to feel strangely uncomfortable. When we finally reached the bottom, she struggled to open a thick metal door, indicating a soundproofed area inside where our group would meet: It was a basement that had been an air raid shelter during World War II! I was stunned. The room seemed filled with fragments of memory, shards of fear, ghosts from the past.

I came to this place eight more times over four years as the training group went through its course. Each time as we walked down those steep stairs into the depths below, it was as if we went down, down into memory and deep into the unconscious. Gradually the childhood stories of each participant emerged. These very sturdy, very bright professionals broke into sobs and sometimes even screams as they recounted events from their lives during the war: living in terror of the next air raid siren; the horror of bloodied or dismembered bodies; grieving over dead family members.

Willy, his deep voice trembling uncontrollably, told of searching desperately for shelter as bombs fell. Anna described how, as sirens sounded, her grandparents rushed with her to the hills surrounding the city, and in the darkness they watched their home go up in flames. Norbert told, in his disconnected monotone, that while he was in his mother's womb she received word that her pilot husband died when his plane was shot down over the ocean. Two-year-old Beate was buried under bedclothes in the cart her mother frantically pushed as she fled their East German estate as Russians advanced. She was told repeatedly and desperately, "Don't you dare make a sound!" Thirty-five years later the terror could still be seen frozen in Beate's large, round, unblinking eyes.

On and on the stories went. And as I heard them I felt almost unbearable pain. Those were *our* planes, *our* bombs! At times it was all I could do to maintain my composure. Sometimes I didn't. At night I lay awake for hours, flooded with thoughts of the vast differences of our personal experiences of World War II, theirs and mine, and the awful reality of war itself. In the group there was no discussion of the politics of the time, or who started the war, no reference to concentration camps or allied casualties, never any anger expressed toward the invading country. Just the painful inner journey to open old wounds with the hope of finding healing after all those years.

As the week wore on, all of us in that room felt sheltered by the deep connections made through the naked sharing of pain, sorrow, and occasionally joy. On the last day we walked out through the dense metal door, and slowly up the countless stairs, one by one, until finally reaching daylight.

I boarded the plane for New York, my carry-on bag filled with T-shirts and other small souvenirs, my body weary and my soul and psyche changed forever. As I settled into my seat, I could feel a smile beginning to form on my lips; soon I would be home to gather up my teenaged children and go out for sushi.

Fun—Finally!

Stanley and Linda Grover had divorced several years before, and she had moved to the West Coast. In the summer after I had returned from Ecuador, Stan invited me to come out to Jones Beach where he was starring in an outdoor theater performance of *Finian's Rainbow*. We had been good friends for years. At this event we became an item. In my journal notes I wrote about the relationship:

> *What he has been to me is everything that was missing in the marriage partner. He is opposite, different—feeling, spontaneous, expansive, generous, positive, and joyful. He's been balm, nourishment, excitement, and flow. Wherever the relationship goes, I'm awfully happy and grateful to have this happening in my life now.*

We had delightful times together, socializing with his friends, interacting with his kids. And always there was the delight of hearing his gorgeous singing voice.

At one time Stan was to do a photo shoot for a commercial filmed in Barbados. He invited me to join him there, and I flew down for a long weekend. Another time we met in Acapulco. We always had fun.

About a year into our relationship, Stan auditioned for a major role in a TV series. He won it and moved to Los Angeles where the pilot was being filmed. I visited him there, and we took an adventurous drive down through Tijuana to Rosarita in Baja, California. Then a helicopter ride to Catalina Island. I wondered, should I move to California to be with this man? Appealing . . . but it didn't seem the right choice. Shortly after that, Stan moved in with a woman who was the star of a daytime series. (His kids, with whom I would continue to have occasional contact, never got on well with her, and daughter Cindy told me that she and Jamie and Steven had so wished Stan and I had gotten married.) Sorry, Cindy. Not meant to be!

Stanley died of leukemia in 1997.

While family life was adjusting to major changes—the divorce, the move, my busy work schedule that included international travel—the children were engaging in their everyday lives with lots of energy, much fun, and with the usual ups and downs of teen years to young adulthood. They always had the backing of their beloved grandparents, who were also adjusting to the changes!

The kids with their grandparents

Steve

Steve was enjoying teaching guitar lessons at his alma mater, Dalton School, and working hard at his music. He soon enrolled in Empire State College, taking classes that furthered his musical interests, and eventually got his degree. He also loved being in his own studio apartment.

In January of 1981 he met and began to date a lovely girl named Catherine Cook. She was from a well-to-do family who lived in Glens Falls, New York. Catherine was a student at Syracuse University, with a major in photojournalism. Just a few days after they met, she went to Italy for a semester in Florence. A couple of months later Steve joined her there for Easter vacation. After Catherine flew home in May she moved in with Steve.

Catherine was hired by the famous Japanese photographer, Hiro. She worked for him for a year, and then she was hired as an artistic assistant by Barry Ladigan, a fashion photographer. Catherine traveled with him to many countries while he was shooting photos for British *Vogue* and Italian *Vogue*. Barry photographed Catherine for an edition of Italian *Vogue*, where she appeared on the cover. (What a keepsake that is!)

Steve, meanwhile, had developed a partnership with a young man named John Green. They began doing gigs together around Manhattan. And then in 1983 they went on tour in Norway. It was quite an adventure for them to be performing in nightclubs in various parts of this European country. They had quite a lot of fun and satisfaction—except for one event. Steve was coming out of a bus in Oslo when a car turned a sharp corner and ran into him! Fortunately, *thankfully*, he was not seriously injured—just

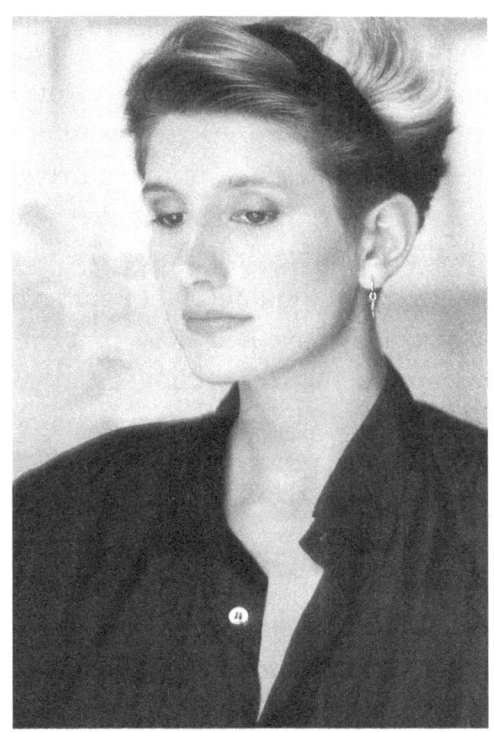

Catherine in Vogue *magazine*

sore and stiff for a while. Steve was glad to get back home to his girlfriend.

In September of 1984 Steve and Catherine were married at Lake George near Glens Falls. A number of family members and friends joined us there for the ceremony in a small chapel near the lake, followed by an elegant reception at the Lake George Country Club. Becca was a bridesmaid and Chris a groomsman. Steve's guitar teacher from tenth grade, Myron Weiss, performed during the beautiful ceremony.

For me, there was a glitch in this moving and meaningful day. At the reception, while Walter and June were seated at the bride's table, I, with my friends and family members, was lost in the middle of the entire crowd. At that point the Cooks may have had some concern about their daughter marrying a musician without a college degree, but I think generally they liked and were accepting of Steve. But I, a divorcée, was a different matter. Susan Cook was skeptical and kept me at arm's length. For the reception, I was placed much more than arm's length away from the bride and groom and other family members! I felt shame and sadness. While in a stall in the ladies' room, I could hear a woman saying to another, "When the groom was dancing with his mother—did you notice how *young* she looks?" Well, that made me feel a *little* better!

(Over time, things got better between Susan Cook and me.)

The best man, Chris

The Marriage Ceremony

Chris

After his graduation from Fieldston School, Chris took a job for the summer at a restaurant on Columbus Avenue. One evening I went there for dinner with a friend of mine. As we had planned, Chris waited on us. As he was about to take our dessert orders with his pad and pencil in hand, a strangely made-up person quickly moved past us and toward the front door. Then someone yelled, *"She's got my purse!"* The person started running. In a flash Chris dropped the pad and pencil and ran after him. (It was immediately apparent that "she" was a "he" in drag!) About half a block down the street Chris caught up with him, and then pinned him to the side of a parked car and held him there. My friend and I, along with other patrons, quickly left the restaurant to see what was happening. Fortunately, the police showed up within a couple of minutes and handcuffed the purse thief. Chris showed them where the guy had bitten him.

"You must go to the ER and have that checked out," the officer ordered. "You'll need a tetanus shot!"

"Okay, but right now I have to get back to my job," Chris replied. He ran back into the restaurant, came over to our table, and picked up the pad and pencil.

"And what may I get you for dessert?" he asked.

We felt certain that this story would be all over the tabloids the next day. But not so. It was July 29, 1981, the day of the wedding of Prince Charles and Lady Diana.

Yet another memorable event took place at this restaurant. Chris was serving a guest who asked him, "Do you know the Hardy Boys stories?"

"Sure," he replied.

"You look like a Hardy Boy. I work at the publishing company for the books, and I'm looking for someone to appear on the cover of the next editions. Would you like to come to my office and we'll discuss this?"

"I'd be glad to!" Chris replied.

He went, and he was hired. He appeared as one of the two Hardy Boys on the cover of a number of books in the series.

Chris chose to go to Wesleyan University. On an early September morning Walter came by to drive him to Middletown, Connecticut. As Chris and I were walking through the lobby on the way to the car, he looked over at me and said with surprise, "Mom, you're crying!" Yes, I was. My second son was leaving home. And going away to college.

Several weeks later I went to Wesleyan for Parents' Day, and enjoyed seeing the campus, the housing, and some of Chris's new friends. I spent part of the day hanging out with another parent, Joanna Carson—Johnny Carson's wife—whose son was one of Chris's housemates.

Chris began an active life at Wesleyan. In addition to his studies, with the focus of American Studies, Chris became a DJ on the campus radio station. He eventually formed a band that performed at the school and in the area.

More Trips with Rebecca

In the summer when Becca was thirteen, she and I went on a short trip to Bermuda. The streets were full of motorbikes. I was terrified, but she had a blast! She soon rode like a pro, easily navigating the crowds of bikers jamming the roadways. We had good mother-daughter time, which we needed, because there had been a lot of tension between us during this difficult period of change for us both. When we returned home she began preparing for another change: She would be graduating to Fieldston School, Ethical Culture's high school. This meant farther to travel on a daily basis, but lots of new friends. She loved it!

When Becca was sixteen, I took her and her friend, Ruthie, to Jamaica during a winter break. We had a rough drive to JFK after a heavy snowstorm, and boarded a small Caribbean Airlines plane. Finally, after many hours of travel in the air and a long jeep ride on the ground, we arrived at our inn on the beach. The girls began to have a blast. They loved swimming in the warm water, and wandering along the beautiful sandy beach. However, they soon found they had to be careful. One night, after everyone was settled in bed, there was pounding on the door. Becca and Ruthie had been followed home by two stoned Rastafarians! On another evening we attended a fantastic reggae concert featuring Rita Marley (Bob Marley's wife).

On our way back to the US, as we were going through the Kingston airport, a woman in uniform grabbed Ruthie and pulled her behind a screen. Becca began to scream, "Mom, they've got Ruthie!" We waited anxiously, and soon they released a terrified girl. "She's okay," the woman said, matter-of-factly. Apparently, something about the way she was dressed had caused concern about whether she was hiding cannabis. We hurried to board the plane, and when Ruthie could feel safe again the two teenagers began an excited conversation, reflecting on their week's happy adventures in Jamaica.

Soon after we returned home it was time once more for me to head off to teach in Germany. I went to JFK for an overnight flight, and when I got to the gate, the attendant looked at my passport, then said sternly, "You can't board the plane. Your passport has expired! You'll have to have it renewed tomorrow. Hopefully we'll find you a seat on tomorrow night's flight." And fortunately, they did. I went back to my apartment, which was empty, since Becca, as usual, was to stay with Walter and June while I was away.

I went to bed early, hoping to get in a good night's sleep, in spite of the stress. Then, in the middle of the night I was jolted awake by the sound of a slammed door and excited voices! *What's happening?* Into my bedroom came Becca and two of her friends.

"Mom!" she shrieked. "What are you doing here?"

"What are *you* doing here?" I replied sternly.

I never found out the exact truth about where they had been until three in the morning. But clearly the girls had contrived a story to assure the parents that they would be safely and appropriately ensconced in one of their homes. My expired passport had ruined their final plans for a whole night on their own.

My children and I were undergoing major changes in our lives. And each had a range of feelings regarding the changes—and the challenges. While I don't want to play down the impact of it all on their lives, in general, the children seemed to be dealing well with the way things were in our family life. As for me, I was happy to have both the changes and the challenges. At the same time, however, I was feeling insecure and anxious about what lay ahead for me. Would I ever have the relationship I longed for? Or would I be alone for the rest of my life?

I continued my commitment to my "inner journey," working hard on feelings and issues related to past and present.

My naughty daughter

The Man on the Beach

July 20, 2011

The phone rang early in the morning. "Is this Virginia?"

"Yes."

"This is Chuck."

"Oh! Good morning, Chuck," I said. I hadn't heard that voice with the Boston accent in twenty-five years.

"I just want you to know that you were an angel sent from God. You saved my life!"

One morning in the summer of 1981, I was at LaGuardia airport waiting for the plane to Boston for a teaching weekend when I ran into my friend, Ann. She was also going there on business. We managed to get seats together on the plane and enjoyed sharing the latest goings-on in our lives.

Ann, a writer as well as a TV producer at the time, was also very involved in Bioenergetic therapy. I often met her at the Loft, the Bioenergetic Institute's meeting space, when she attended events there, including exercise classes that I taught. She lived on the Upper West Side, and we often took the subway home together after Tuesday night seminars and other meetings. On the ride to Boston she told me that on Saturday night she would be driving down toward Plymouth on Cape Cod to have dinner with her favorite cousin, Chuck. Would I like to come along?

Sure, I said. Why not?

After my workshop was over Ann picked me up and we drove the hour or so to meet her cousin at a restaurant, and we began a pleasant evening with Bloody Marys, followed by good food and wine.

Chuck was a fifty-seven-year-old dentist. He was divorced, had four children, and was part of a large clan of Scots whose forebears had come to Nova Scotia a couple of generations before. He was short and stocky, with a jovial smile, and a strong Boston accent. As the evening wore on it was clear that he was a smart, charming, and easygoing guy.

After dinner we followed Chuck to his apartment, had an after-dinner drink, and spent another hour chatting. Ann and her cousin reminisced about family gatherings while I listened, sometimes with interest, sometimes wandering off into my own thoughts. Then, as I was looking at Chuck's face during the pleasant banter, I suddenly felt an inner jolt.

A few months before, I had attended an EST seminar, or "training," as it was called. Ann had been the inspiration. During one session the participants were instructed in a guided imagery process. After a few minutes I saw in my mind's eye a beautiful beach in a tropical location, waves gently rolling ashore. At one end of the sandy beach there was a hut, or cabana. And as I breathed in the salt air and the peacefulness of the surroundings, I saw a man emerge from the cabana. As I watched him walk slowly toward me I thought, "This is the man I'm waiting for in my life!" It had been four years since my marriage had come to an end. It was time. Suddenly, as Ann and her cousin continued their conversation, my sleepy eyes widened and my jaw dropped. Chuck looked just like that man on the beach! A few minutes later Chuck followed us to the car and we said goodbye. I could sense that he was attracted to me. Perhaps he also sensed the change in me, brought about by my sudden revelation.

Two days later he called me in New York and invited me to come back to Boston the following weekend. I did. And that began the weekly foray, one or the other of us traveling back and forth to meet for the weekend. There was a strong attraction between us. He was bright and congenial and fun. When he came to New York we would go immediately to a restaurant, have Bloody Marys, and a relaxed evening. It was a great relief from my busy life of practice, and relief from the stress of being a single mom raising a teenaged daughter.

The weekends in this rather rural part of Massachusetts were welcomed getaways. Chuck moved to a small house on a lake, and I enjoyed being in nature when I wasn't conducting my training seminars in Boston. We could have continued our relationship in that manner, but Chuck may have been uncomfortable to openly engage in a non-marital alliance. And I felt it would be good for my children for me to have a "settled" life. So, only a few months after we met, we began talking about marriage, and soon we were planning a Thanksgiving wedding.

Chuck went with me to Texas to meet my parents. He was no Walter, but they liked him, and I think were relieved that their divorced daughter would no longer be single. Chuck was a terrible driver, occasionally going off the road slightly or unaware of what other cars were doing. On the way back to the Houston airport he put us in total jeopardy when he ran through a stop sign, and a fast-moving car barely avoided crashing into us.

Our wedding took place in Newport, Rhode Island, in one of the seaside mansions converted into a hotel. My parents, our children, and many friends from New York attended. Ann, Chuck's cousin and my friend, was my maid of honor. I wore the deep blue velvet dress my mother had worn at her own wedding in 1932.

I don't know exactly when Chuck informed me of his financial state. I was horrified to learn that he hadn't paid income taxes for several years. He was deeply in debt. He and his dental partner owned a property with a large wooden Cape Cod style house that was rented out to a couple who put a small restaurant on the ground floor. They were struggling and paid very little rent. The dental practice was in a small building on the property. The two men were relieved to have their mortgage loan renewed—at about a 30 percent interest rate! Chuck said that a high percentage of his patients owed him money for his services. He was clearly a good dentist and had taught at the dental school in Boston, but apparently, he wasn't good at business.

We found an attractive house for rent in Marshfield, and I furnished a basement room for an office where I could see a few clients when I was there. I paid the rent.

Chris was at that time attending Wesleyan University in Connecticut. He borrowed Chuck's old station wagon one weekend when he was doing a gig with his newly formed

New England wedding

band. There was an accident and the car was damaged. I paid for a new car.

The following September, ten months after our wedding, I was in Massachusetts for the first training weekend of the season. After I arrived on Friday evening Chuck and I went to dinner with his very likeable daughter, Donna, who was visiting for the weekend. After the usual evening of cocktails, food, and wine, we came back to our home, and I, preparing for a busy day of teaching, went to bed. Chuck and Donna stayed in the study and continued talking, laughing—and drinking. About one o'clock I was awakened when Chuck came into the room in the dark and made a loud noise as he bumped into a chair.

"What's the matter? What are you doing?" I asked, startled, but only half awake.

In a voice I had never heard before he replied, "Don't talk to me like that!" He was drunk. And angry. I was stunned.

When I returned home at the end of the day on Saturday, I found that Chuck remembered nothing from the night before. He had been in a blackout. I said nothing at the time and went back to New York in a grim state. There had been, of course, clear signs all along of too much drinking. But nothing like this. I had never seen him drunk. And I had never experienced anger in him, let alone the sound of viciousness that came out in the dark.

During the following week I had a consultation with a substance abuse expert. The session confirmed the conclusion I had reached by the time I left Marshfield. When Chuck came to New York the following week I told him that I would not stay in the marriage unless he went to Alcoholics Anonymous and quit drinking entirely. He said goodbye, drove to Boston, and went straight to an AA meeting. As far as I know he never touched another drop of alcohol.

But that's not the whole story. Around the time of our first anniversary I went to Amsterdam to teach. Chuck met me there. At dinner with a colleague and his wife one evening, our host, Jan Velzeboer, poured Chuck a glass of fine wine. Chuck smiled and said, "No thank you. I've had more than my share." Our dinners changed rather radically. I limited my alcohol intake, or abstained in support. When in Massachusetts I went along to AA meetings instead of our cheerful evenings out. Yet, what a relief!

I urged Chuck to go into therapy, but he had no interest. He believed that his intelligence and his religion were all that were needed. His money problems got no better. While I had thought initially that I would eventually leave New York City and live full-time in Massachusetts, it became clear that I was the one who was supporting us with a solid income. The only reasonable solution was for him to join me in New York. He was verbally agreeable to this. Yet, as the weeks and months passed, he never showed indications of inquiring about possible locations for practice.

In spring of 1983, my humorous male accountant, after preparing my income tax report, looked at me and said, "Virginia, you sure are paying a lot of money to get laid on the weekends!"

In May of '83, I happened to be in Austin, Texas doing a training weekend. Before I had left New York, I had had some conversations with my son, Steve, who had begun working for a real estate firm. I, along with a long-time friend, Thayer Greene, had been talking with him about investing in property. (Even with all the extra expenses, I had managed to save a fair amount of my teaching income.) All the financial signs seemed to indicate that it was a good time to invest in real estate. During a long night-time phone call with Chuck I told him about my interest and potential plans. He erupted. "I thought you would use your money for an office for me!" he shouted. Again, I was stunned. No alcohol this time, but no change. I reflected painfully through the night, particularly on the lack of motivation or movement on his part to explore professional possibilities. Was he really willing to move to New York?

By the time I returned home I had faced some hard realities. Chuck was a very dear man with a good heart, and our time together had been in many ways pleasurable and a respite from the stresses of my life. But he and I were very different people, living in very different worlds. (This had indeed struck me, I remembered with humor, on his very first visit to NYC, when he showed up in his tweed suit with a Rotary pin on his lapel.) And he had been unwilling to deal with the issues underlying the alcoholism that were undermining his life. What must I do? I was forty-eight years old! Face the possibility of being alone the rest of my life? Accept the shame of acknowledging to family and colleagues and clients that the marriage was a mistake? *Damn, that stupid EST experience!*

When Chuck arrived in New York the following weekend, I simply said to him:

"I love you and care about you, but I don't want to be married to you anymore." He immediately took off his ring and handed it to me. *That must have been a relief to him, somehow.* Then he said goodbye, turned and left the apartment. The next weekend Steve and I drove to

Marshfield with a U-haul, loaded my stuff, and drove back to the city.

In the evening on the 4th of July I met my good friend, Jane Downs, at a sushi restaurant on 57th St. I was sad and somewhat bereft, and talked about the events of the past weeks. And then the two of us walked across town to the East River for the magnificent fireworks display. Gradually the exhilaration of the gleeful crowds of onlookers, the exploding light and sound that built to the glorious climax, changed the mood. Who knew what the future held, what the possibilities would be?

But I was back on track.

July 20, 2011

Several days before I had been rummaging through old papers and souvenirs, and I came across a letter that Chuck had written to me while we were married. He spoke kindly about my children, and I was touched by the warmth of it. Serendipitously, I had a phone conversation with Ann's sister, Jan. She had told me previously that Chuck mentioned to her how he hoped to talk with me again someday. I told Jan about the letter I had discovered. "I'd be glad to talk with Chuck," I said to her.

And then the next morning he called. After his startling greeting we chatted a bit about our children, and he indicated that he was happy in his current marriage and his life. And then he said, "Angels don't have to stay around. They do their thing, and then they go on. . . ."

Completion.

Two years later, in the spring of 2015, Chuck passed away. Again, I got a call from Jan.

"We are at Chuck's memorial. His kids are here and they want to speak to you." So, one by one, the three daughters and one son, with whom I hadn't had contact in more than thirty years, got on the phone and thanked me—for saving their father's life.

The Pearl of Great Price

In the fall of 1983 I was eagerly anticipating the annual faculty meeting of IIBA, that year to be held in Old Saybrook on the Connecticut shore. I arrived at the hotel and was at the desk checking in when I saw Bob Hilton looking down from the top of the staircase. I gasped for breath. We had seen each other at conferences almost yearly since we met ten years before. But now for the first time we were both single!

Bob had learned from Al Lowen that my marriage hadn't worked out, and he was anticipating seeing me at Old Saybrook. Later he commented to friends, "When I saw her looking up at me, I said to myself, I think I'm about to buy the Brooklyn Bridge!"

We took a walk on the beach before the meeting started, then later we drove to a nearby restaurant for a lovely dinner. Bob ordered salmon, which arrived overdone, and he immediately sent it back to the kitchen. I was quite impressed by this. That was not behavior to which I was accustomed. Hmmm. Both of us enjoyed the evening—which ended with a beautiful kiss. The next day we parted ways, with the clear intention of staying in touch by telephone.

And staying in touch we did. The following evening Bob called from California. We talked for a long time, sharing views regarding the meeting and recalling the time spent together. The next day I called him. A female voice answered the phone. *What? Does he have a live-in girlfriend?* I panicked. When he returned my call, he told me that his oldest daughter was visiting. What a relief! I could breathe again.

Soon after, I said to Bob when he telephoned, "I have been lying on the floor, feeling the vibrations as I listen to the recording of Elgar's "Cello Concerto," played magnificently by Jacqueline du Pre. It's such gorgeous music, with tones that descend to the depths. It made me think of our relationship, which I believe has the possibility of that quality and that depth."

Bob liked that observation. His thoughts: "Oh. She's capable of deep feeling!" Our calls became daily. And long. Soon we began to make plans for my coming to California after Christmas.

After the family holiday celebration, I boarded a plane for Los Angeles, leaving my children and a snowstorm behind. When I arrived, what excitement to see Bob moving toward me in the terminal! As we exited the baggage claim area, he commented that his car was parked a long way away. He pointed to a stretch limousine parked at the curb and then added, "Let's take this," as if it were a last-minute decision. The female driver smiled at us and opened the door. We ducked inside, and there was champagne and appetizers, beautifully displayed and ready to be devoured. What a welcome!

Excitement surged during the drive to Irvine. The female driver quietly kept track of what was happening in her rearview mirror.

I was interested and pleased with what I saw along the way, and surprised by the neighborhood as we drove up to 14 Bascom. When we got inside, Tarzan went over to Jane, picked her up, and took her toward the treehouse.

"I have to take a shower!" Jane shrieked. "I was in an airplane for hours!" Tarzan looked surprised—and a little miffed.

"Well, okay," he said, and waited patiently for a few minutes.

Bob prepared a scrumptious dinner that evening. It began with an appetizer: boursin cheese on water crackers with caviar. Then French onion soup, made from scratch. Then Caesar salad with homemade dressing, and tournedos and asparagus. For dessert there was orange sorbet topped with grand marnier and pirouettes. (As I learned later, all recipes were from the *Playboy Cookbook*. Wow!)

The next morning we drove to Palm Springs where we spent three nights at an elegant hotel. It was amazing being poolside during the day—at the end of December! On New Year's Eve there was a banquet at the hotel, and we were assigned to a table with another couple, the only Black people in the room. We enjoyed talking with them. But after a time Bob wanted to go to another part of the hotel to dance, so we left them and didn't return. (I would forever regret this. We abandoned them at our table on New Year's Eve!)

On New Year's Day we returned to Orange County. We went for lunch at a restaurant called the "Rusty Pelican," on the bay in Newport Beach. I was thrilled to walk on the sandy shore in ninety-degree weather. (I would later learn that the warmth was due to what is called Santa Ana conditions—desert winds blowing from the north.) I was in heaven! (Later Bob would say he didn't know for sure whether it was he or the weather that persuaded me to move to California.)

In February of '84, I came back to California, this time with my daughter, who was considering attending UC Berkeley. By that time it was clear that, while there was a lot of excitement between us, Bob also had some ambivalence regarding the relationship. He would be there fully with lots of feeling, and then he would tighten and withdraw. I had experienced this while we were in Palm Springs. I had said to him that, in my past if I felt a person was not fully present, fully into the relationship, then I was out. But this time I felt there were true possibilities in what existed between us, and I wasn't going to run. And now during the second visit, while we were at the beach, the ambivalence was showing up again. On the weekend Bob was meeting with his "advanced group," trainees he'd been instructing since 1979. He was looking forward to introducing me. I said to him that I could not do that if he was uncertain about the relationship. I would go back home.

We went back to the house to prepare for an evening trip to Los Angeles. I was blow-drying my hair after a shower when Bob came into the bathroom and looked at my face in the mirror. He could see the hurt, the sorrow, and the deep disappointment at not having his love. He fell down to the floor and began to sob.

"I've never in my life seen a look like that—someone's pain at not having me."

Bob's early years were filled with abandonment. As we both learned through our therapy training and practice, such trauma called for a protective shield against the pain of loss. His shield was saying, "Never again—don't open to love, or you'll be abandoned again—and you may die!" When Bob saw the pain and the caring in my eyes, it opened a crack in the shield. He didn't want to lose me. We embraced with all the feelings inside us both.

And then, bringing Becca with us, we drove to Los Angeles to see the production of *The Torch Song Trilogy*.

Several months later, Bob came for a long weekend, his first visit to my home. I met him at the airport, and we drove back to begin experiencing the best of New York City. Besides trips to museums, I had purchased tickets for two Broadway plays: Tom Stoppard's *The Real Thing* (with Jeremy Irons and Glenn Close) and August Wilson's *Ma Rainey's Black Bottom*. We loved them both. I got a reservation at a very popular, fine-dining restaurant that was a favorite of the stars, "The Quilted Giraffe." On another night we explored a well-known dinner destination on the river near the Brooklyn Bridge. We had much pleasure and fun, which further increased the closeness between us. Saying goodbye was growing harder and harder. And the phone calls were daily—and longer.

In May the annual IIBA faculty meeting was held at Grossinger's, the iconic hotel in the Catskills. As with all the faculty meetings of the past ten years, we both attended. But now we were a couple. It was the first time our relationship was made public to our professional community. We got a lot of positive feedback for our dancing—and had a great time.

There was, however, a difficult issue that reared its head at that time, and would take quite a while to be resolved. One night when we were in our room, the phone rang. It was Bob's ex-wife. She had some problem that kept him on the phone for a very long time. I became quite restless, then angry. Why was he paying attention to her and not me? After all, she's his *ex*.

During late August I went back to California hoping for a genuine vacation. Bob and I drove up to Lake Arrowhead and stayed for a few days at the home owned by his former neighbors, the Aldersons. Soon after we arrived he began doing Bioenergetic exercises, and working on personal issues. His goal was to be authentic, to present himself as he really was, not the narcissistic version. I appreciated this, but my own need was to rest and relax.

"Can't we just go for a walk, smell the flowers?" I pleaded. We finally did get to wander through the woods and around the lake, and we enjoyed dancing at the Lake Arrowhead Resort (where we also received lots of compliments).

We came back to Orange County and spent two nights at the Surf and Sand Hotel in Laguna Beach. This soon became a favorite "go-to" place for a brief vacation (before they upgraded the hotel and it became quite expensive).

When I came back to New York, Becca was busily preparing to go to California to begin college at UC Berkeley. The problem was, I had just spent two weeks in California, and I had to get back to my practice. I would be leaving again soon, and I couldn't go with Becca. (What unfortunate timing! This girl had already experienced too many lonely plane rides. And what about settling in to new quarters?)

Walter and June put her on the plane, and I spent a sleepless night worrying about her trip and all that was ahead. With a few difficulties along the way, she finally was ensconced in her off-campus living place, which she came to love.

While the direction of my life was not yet certain, I was so happy that Becca would be in California.

In September Bob came back to New York for a weekend. Among other things we spent a romantic evening at "Windows on the World," the beautiful restaurant at the top of the Twin Towers. (Seventeen years later, amidst the horror, we would remember that night with sorrow and anguish as the Towers came crashing down.)

Back in my apartment, we began addressing issues between us. Bob's ambivalence had returned—or persisted. I suggested we use our Bioenergetic techniques to get to withheld feelings. We each stood at one end of the bed in my office and used tennis rackets to release the anger. We both hit the bed hard, yelled, and got out the frustrations. I said to him, "Are you going to go back to your lonely house, get in your huge bed, and cover yourself with your black bedspread? And stay that way forever?"

I was very sad. It seemed the relationship was over. We said goodbye and Bob headed for the airport.

I had several really tough days. It was hard to believe. It had seemed so right. And now I felt so very alone. My boys were living their own lives, my daughter was in college, and this relationship—which was everything I had wanted—had walked out the door. Now what? I couldn't even think.

In the middle of the week the phone rang. It was Bob. "I'm going to take the red-eye tomorrow night. I'll be back in New York early Friday morning . . . is that okay?"

Virginia Wink Hilton

Windows on the World

There was silence for a moment. I was speechless. "You're coming back? Friday? Are you sure?"

"Yes, I'm very sure. I can't wait to get back to you."

"Nor can I," was my barely audible reply.

Early Friday morning I was still in my nightgown when the doorbell rang. I flung on my kimono bathrobe and opened the door. There he was, so early in the morning. We had a very long embrace. Bob maneuvered me into my office and over to my desk. He then fell to his knees and held out his hand.

"Virginia," he said. "Will you marry me?"

I threw my arms around him and began to sob while saying softly, "Yes, I will!"

A short while later we left the apartment to go shopping—for an engagement ring! At a Winston Jewelry we found a lovely ring with the right-sized diamond. Bob was elated, and so was I. And I kept thinking, *Is this really happening?*

"You know what?" he asked. "Al Lowen is leading a workshop this very day in a hotel that's just a few blocks away. Let's go find him!"

We found the hotel, and walked into the meeting room just as the group was breaking for lunch. Al was both surprised and pleased to see us.

"Al," Bob said, "We have great news to tell you. I arrived in New York this morning on a red-eye flight from LA to ask Virginia to marry me—and she said, 'Yes!'" Al was clearly pleased to hear this.

"Congratulations to you both," he said. "I've been hoping things would go this way."

"If it weren't for you this wouldn't have happened," Bob said. And that was true. "You remember we met at the Aspen conference more than ten years ago?"

"Yes. Well, it's about time!" Al replied.

I showed him the engagement ring, and he smiled and gave a warm hug to each of us. How synchronous that we could have these moments with him on this very special day!

Receiving Al Lowen's blessing

California, Here I Come— For Good!

As I moved through my forties, I found myself thinking that to live in New York City one should be either young or rich. Preferably both. Since I was neither, what should I do? I decided that, because I had already been teaching training groups there, Boston and San Francisco were good possibilities. And I loved both places. Especially San Francisco. Then came my relationship with Bob. And now I was moving to California! Not the Bay Area, but Orange County. I was elated.

Of course, there was sadness about leaving New York— my home for twenty-five years—my kids, my clients, my colleagues, my therapists, my friends. It would not be an easy transition. But the Big Apple would always be just a plane ride away.

I began to inform my clients that I would be closing my New York practice and moving to California in the spring. Most were understanding, though sad, as was I, to end our professional relationship. One of them, a woman who lived in Boston, on hearing the news replied with anger and tears, "Why are you doing that? You've been married enough!"

On March 10, 1985, my long-time friend, Jane Downs, hosted a farewell party for me. Many people attended, colleagues, friends, clients, my children. It was a lovely and very moving send-off.

Among those who came with cards and letters was John Collins, who was a long-time member of one of my therapy groups. He brought with him a poem about his experience in the group:

Virginia Wink
PRESENTE!

"Who wants to work?"
The dreaded, yet eagerly awaited question, is spoken.
It is Monday afternoon, just 28 minutes before the 6 o'clock news, as the soft Texas voice opens Pandora's box once again.
For the next ninety minutes, this 20th century witch with healing
In her heart will guide this ragged group of pilgrims through the perils of purgatory.
This sanctuary (place of refuge and protection) resounds with screams, moans, rage, curses, copious tears, and vicious tennis strokes that make even John McEnroe seem good-natured by comparison.
Fearful memories, old hatreds, lost loves, emerge at this weekly dusk, bidden or unbidden, possessing those who have for so long
possessed them.

And somehow, in that holy place and in this company, these demons
are met, named, faced, and if not cast out, at least cut down to size.
Amid these storms, this tumult, these dangers and these floods of
tears, sits cross-legged and quixotic this small woman, this minister of Kleenex, possessor of great medicine, riding the waves and currents with the ease of a skilled surfer.
And we know, without ever pausing to ask or look, that she is, for
each of those 5400 seconds . . . intensely, watchfully, lovingly, Patiently, powerfully, fully . . . present.

John Collins
pilgrim
March 10, 1985

Needless to say, this was a deeply appreciated acknowledgment, and a most gracious gift to send me on my way.

I went about the task of sorting and arranging the items I would take with me to California, and preparing the apartment for Chris who would be returning from college. His best friend from high school, Matt Goldman, would move in with him. To my great delight the apartment would become the meeting place on Sundays for a group of friends who discussed their interest in art and theater and other creative pursuits. Phil Stanton would join, and eventually Chris, Matt, and Phil would combine their talents and skills to create Blue Man Group. *Hooray, hooray!*

Moving day finally arrived. I could hardly believe it.

Who was this man I was going to marry?

Bob was born in Los Angeles in 1932. His grandparents had come to California from Indiana around 1930. Their sixteen-year-old daughter, Lilian, the only one who could find work, was a waitress at Gibson's Café. She became pregnant by the eighteen-year-old dishwasher. And twelve days after her seventeenth birthday she gave birth to Bobby—who never saw his father.

When Bob was twelve, Lilian married Bill Hilton, who lived on a ranch in Lancaster in the High Desert. Bill had two sons, the older of which died from a burst appendix at age eighteen. Bob was fifteen, and he, too, had serious abdominal pain. He feared he was going to die, as Billy had. As a result, he had a religious experience that changed the course of his life. The local Baptist church welcomed him, and soon he was actually preaching! In 1950 the pastor encouraged him to go to Bethel, a college affiliated with the Baptist General Conference, founded by the Swedish Baptist Church, in St. Paul, Minnesota. In 1954 he entered Fuller Seminary in Pasadena, and in 1955 he married Pat, his girlfriend during the Bethel years. In 1956 their daughter, Kathy, was born.

After he finished seminary, Bob became the pastor of Cochran Avenue Baptist Church in Los Angeles (which was located close to where he had lived during his very early life). In 1961 he began teaching homiletics and pastoral counseling at the California Baptist Seminary in Covina, and at the same time entered Claremont School of Theology for his PhD, which he received in 1965, along with a license to practice psychotherapy. A year earlier he went to Esalen Institute in Big Sur for a long week to learn about Gestalt therapy, and there he was "born again" into the humanistic movement.

In 1967 Bob left the ministry, the professorship, and his marriage. He moved to Orange County where he began a private practice in psychotherapy in Santa Ana. In 1968, he met Renato Monaco, a psychiatrist who became his close friend and partner. The two of them would establish the Southern California Institute for Bioenergetic Analysis. Renato introduced Bob to a young woman, Peni, who would become his wife in 1975. They had two children, and were divorced in 1982.

In April 1985, as the plane was descending after the cross-country flight, I looked out the window with wonder at the expanse of hills, buildings, homes, freeways, and in the distance, the Pacific Ocean. "I'm not coming for a visit," I marveled to myself. "I'm about to land at my new home!" Unbelievable.

Bob greeted me with affection and enthusiasm. On the hour's drive to Irvine I took note of everything along the way. As we drove up to the house on Bascom St., I looked at it, too, with different eyes. A new life was beginning.

We walked into the house at about nine o'clock in the evening. No sooner had I set my carry-ons down than the phone rang. It was Bob's ex-wife. I sat quietly and took some deep breaths while he talked, wondering why it was taking so long. When he finally hung up Bob told me that she was very upset. Then a short time later, with some annoyance he said he had to check in with her again. Oh, dear. This was not what either of us had expected for my first night in my new home.

Several days later when we went to pick up Bob's two daughters and take them out to dinner, I was quite struck by how attractive—and young—their mother was.

Eight-year-old Tayne and five-year-old Tara were wearing fancy dresses and shiny patent leather shoes. They sat in the back seat of the car with their legs straight out in front of them, being rather silent, wondering what to think of this unknown woman in the front seat. We drove to Coco's, the restaurant Bob frequented with them (where adults could have wine).

Tayne was a sweet and beautiful child, much loved by her parents, who one day would develop and practice the skills she had inherited from her father. Tara had been born with a hydrocephalic condition that sadly limited her life. She inherited artistic talent from her mother's side, and Bob often referred to her as having a beautiful soul.

I was happy to get to know these dear ones, my stepdaughters-to-be. (It would be a while before I had the privilege of meeting Bob's delightful daughter, Kathy, who was living in Martha's Vineyard.) Tayne and Tara would stay with us every other weekend and each Wednesday night. I soon discovered that Bob had a very rigid and limited schedule with the girls. I felt they needed adventure on the weekends—*I* certainly did—so immediately I began planning trips to interesting places. In addition to Knott's Berry Farm and Disney Land, we enjoyed such things as riding horses at Warner Springs Ranch, and hiking on Catalina Island.

In spite of their initial moans and groans, the girls responded quite positively to visits to LACMA—Los Angeles County Museum of Art—and occasionally the Bowers Museum in Orange County. The next Christmas we took them with us to Timberline Lodge on Mt. Hood, where they had a ski lesson—and got to see real live reindeer outside the hotel.

Tayne and Tara

On Catalina Island

After a couple of years, the girls' mother got remarried and moved to El Segundo. While we drove Tayne and Tara back home after their weekend stays with us, we always listened to Garrison Keillor on *Prairie Home Companion*. All four of us became avid fans.

A number of years later Tayne and I would be excited to drive to the Greek Theater and sit in the front row for a live performance by Garrison Keillor and his show.

Bob and Renato Monaco shared an office in Newport Beach, and I was able to rent space nearby. Renato referred my first client, the wife of one of his patients. She arrived in her white Mercedes convertible, wearing an off-the-shoulder blouse, a short skirt, and high heels. After beginning remarks and information, I introduced her to my "opening and grounding" exercises. At one point she was bending forward, and suddenly she began to cry. I gently asked her what she was feeling. Her response, in the midst of tears, was, "I just had a *really* bad shopping day!" My silent response was: *Oh, dear God, I've died and gone to hell!*

The next new client asked me if I would please pray with her at the end of each session. Gradually, the right clients—and friends—found their way to my door.

Bob commented to a client of his that his fiancée had begun a "little practice." (I think he had a fantasy of my waiting at the door for him at the end of each day, wine and homemade appetizer in hand. Eventually, though, Bob and I moved into a shared office in Costa Mesa, and my practice grew to full-time. He was actually quite pleased about that!)

After only a month in California it was time for me to fly to Norway for two weeks of teaching. Bob drove me to LAX and we said goodbye, sad to be parting so soon. Once inside the terminal, with Bob long gone, I discovered that I had not put my billfold in my purse! Fortunately, I did have my passport.

What am I going to do? No money. No money at all! The airline did provide an evening meal, but the flight was many hours long, and there were lots of hungry minutes. Then an amazing thing happened: During a brief layover in Copenhagen, I ran into the very man who had invited me to teach in Bergen, and who was to be my host as well. He was on his way back to his home. He gave me money for a meal, and later paid my fee in cash before I even started teaching. Problem solved. (Whew!)

The next morning, I telephoned Bob. He had just come into the house after his long day of work. "What the . . ." I heard him almost shout. "Your jewelry is all over the bed! Damn! We've been robbed!" There was a pause. Then he said soberly, "Looks like they emptied the jewelry drawer on the bed and took the old gold wedding rings and some other valuable stuff." Another pause. "And they took your gold coins!"

A couple of years before I left New York, and out of concern about the future of the stock market, I invested some savings in International Year of the Child Commemorative Coins. A box full of engraved gold coins sat on my lap during the flight to California. Bob didn't think it was necessary to put them in a safety deposit box after I arrived. He had no concern about robbery. "After all," he said, "we live in the safest city in the country!"

That day when he went to his office, he had left the back door unlocked. A teenaged boy, who was living temporarily next door to us and spent most days skateboarding around the block, was the likely suspect. But we never knew what happened.

A tough start on my trip to Norway, and such disturbing news on my first day! But after that, I had a wonderful time with the training group in Bergen, the magnificent train ride to Oslo, and a great week of teaching and sightseeing in that beautiful city.

When I returned home, the good news was that Bob had insurance that covered a lot of what was stolen, including the coin collection. We took that money and bought a piano. Hooray!

* * *

Bob and I first planned to get married in the fall of '85. Al Lowen had told Bob about a place he loved on the beach in Puerto Vallarta, Mexico: Garza Blanca. We thought that would be a great place for a honeymoon, so we made reservations. Then we decided to postpone the wedding until later. But we kept the reservation and flew to Puerto Vallarta in October—for an early honeymoon.

When we arrived at Garza Blanca, we left our belongings in the lovely villa on the beach, and then walked on the sand back to the terrace restaurant. There we indulged in chips and salsa, a full dinner, and constantly refilled margaritas. Well after dark we started back down the path to our villa, and halfway there we ended up lying on the sand, under a million stars, while the waves flowed in and out. (Passersby might have thought they were observing a scene from the movie *From Here to Eternity*.)

As the days and weeks passed, I became more and more adjusted to my new home. I learned more about my surroundings, my friends, and my clients. And the relationship with Bob grew wider and deeper each day. Yet there was an area of difficulty: his unfinished issues with his much younger ex-wife. As was demonstrated on the night of my move-in, she would periodically contact him with a need of some sort, often at inconvenient times (as when we were at Grossinger's, and again at another conference in Belgium). I was very annoyed by these calls, and I wondered why he continued to respond, why he hadn't drawn the line in the sand. It was as though he was the parent—or the therapist—when she experienced a problem or need. (Bob explained to me later that the attachment that remained was indeed due to the early childhood traumas they both had experienced, and the transference and countertransference that was present from the beginning of their relationship.)

In January of 1986 we had a meeting with our couples' group—colleagues and their wives who lived in the area. I was able to express my concern about Bob's interactions with his former wife. Our friends gave support to each of us for expressing our anger: mine toward Bob, and his toward his ex. Later that night, after everyone had returned home, we got several calls from our friends, asking with concern about how we were doing. They were worried about the state of our relationship. Was it over? No way! I felt enormous relief, and so did Bob, after bringing the issue into the open, and especially for expressing the frustration and rage. We looked at each other with new respect. And the love deepened.

The Wedding

We began to plan our wedding, scheduled for April 6, 1986. Bob's close friends and colleagues, who had been meeting twice a year since 1979 (and were known as the "79ers"), were scheduled to meet in the Bay Area in the spring of 1986. Why not get married there so they could all be with us? We decided to have the wedding at the home of Bob's close buddy, David Finlay, who lived in Larkspur, above San Francisco in Marin County. I asked Eugenia Gerard, who had become a close friend since our meeting during the sabbatical stay in Berkeley in '72, to be my matron of honor. David was to be Bob's best man. The 79ers arrived in Berkeley from different states the day before, and that night we had a lovely dinner and a boisterous celebration.

The next day everyone, including my daughter, Rebecca, made their way to Larkspur for the wedding. It took place in the outside patio of David's home. Paul Oas, a Bioenergetic colleague and an ordained minister, performed the ceremony.

At the pre-wedding party

The ceremony

The Sermon

"The impetus for this special day was elicited by Bob and Virginia's experience of grace, graciousness, and especially gratitude. In my attempt to synthesize the years, events, and people that have combined to form this day, three words describe our experience—and now this couple: Grace, Graciousness, and Gratitude.

Grace—Bob and Virginia, the first recollection of grace associated with your relationship was when we watched you dance at Grossinger's two years ago—beautiful, free, flowing, joyful. It was like the pulsation of two protoplasms, each with its own rhythm, its own ebb and flow, touching, then moving as one.

Anne Morrow Lindberg, in her book *Gift from the Sea* wrote:

A good relationship is built on some of the same rules. The partners do not need to hold on tightly, because they move confidently in the same pattern, intricate but gay and swift and free, like a country dance of Mozart's. To touch heavily would be to arrest the pattern and freeze the movement, to check the endlessly changing beauty of its unfolding. There is no place here for the possessive clutch, the clinging arm, the heavy hand; only the barest touch in passing. Now arm in arm, now face to face, now back to back, it does not matter which. Because they know they are partners moving to the same rhythm, creating a pattern together, and being invisibly nourished by it.

It is that of which Blake was speaking when he wrote:

He who bends to himself a joy,
Doth the winged life destroy;
But he who kisses the joy as it flies,
Lives in eternity's sunrise.

Bob and Virginia, you continue to touch each other and us with grace.

A life that has experienced grace expresses itself with <u>graciousness</u>. Graciousness is grace with legs. The grace we saw in the two of you as you floated across the floor ever so gracefully, had a beautiful flowing quality to it—like some ethereal romantic dream, inspiring some of us to fantasize of this day's possibility.

But the grace of that day took on legs and it became bump and grind for two years. A bit of the walk down Calvary road—grace paying its admission to reality.

Bob and Virginia have paid the price of admission. Our love for you both has grown out of your willingness to graciously share your realities, your life process with us.

It is the dance we have all learned to dance, each learning a new step from the other—but ever so compassionately, so graciously.

'Ecstasy' comes from a word meaning 'out of stasis.' But the life filled with the ecstasy of experienced grace and graciousness soon becomes stagnant, were it not for <u>gratitude</u>.

Gratitude is the refractory period, the afterglow which becomes the seed of grace to begin new life, a new cycle. Gratitude is the final signature on a life that is lived in grace, graciously.

While searching for family ties in Norway, I saw on a tombstone what summarized a life that must have known grace, graciousness, and gratitude, for it said simply, Tak for alt—thanks for everything!

It is grace that created this group—this couple.

It is graciousness that has kept us together.

It is gratitude that moves us out together.

Anne Morrow Lindberg quotes Antoine de Saint-Exupéry: 'Love does not consist in gazing at each other, but in looking forward together in the same direction.'

Bob and Virginia, with Grace, Graciousness, and Gratitude we celebrate this day with you. Our love and prayers go with you!"

Paul Oas ended his sermon with the *Apache Benediction*:

Now you will feel no rain, for each of you will be shelter to the other. Now you will feel no cold, for each of you will be warmth to the other. Now there is no loneliness for you. Now you are two persons, but there is one life before you. Go now to your dwelling place to enter into the days of your togetherness. And may your days be good and long together.

Paul then asked the groom what he wanted to say to the bride. Bob recited verbatim—and from memory—his favorite Shakespeare sonnet:

When, in disgrace with fortune and men's eyes,
I all alone beweep my outcast state,
And trouble deaf heaven with my bootless cries,
And look upon myself and curse my fate,
Wishing me like to one more rich in hope,
Featured like him, like him with friends possessed,
Desiring this man's art and that man's scope,
With what I most enjoy contented least;
Yet in these thoughts myself almost despising,
Haply I think on thee, and then my state,
(Like to the lark at break of day arising
From sullen earth) sings hymns at heaven's gate;
For thy sweet love remembered such wealth brings
That then I scorn to change my state with kings.

Everyone was moved. Then Paul asked me what I wanted to say to the groom. That morning, while taking a shower, I had a thought about something humorous I would say, and for some reason the thought stayed with me until the ceremony.

"After twenty-five years in New York, I said goodbye to my clients, my colleagues, and my three children. I gathered together all my little pearls, and came out to California, for the 'pearl of great price.' It is such a joy for me to be here with Bob, with all of you—in my true home. And I have come to know that when you want something with all your heart, it can be yours. What I want now with all my heart—is a jacuzzi!"

There was much laughter all around, including from Bob, though he did look a little dumbfounded. It wasn't the answer he was expecting! And guess what—I never got a jacuzzi. (Turns out, I didn't need it.)

We said our vows, and then we were happily Man and Wife!

I now had the pearl of great price, *and* all I wanted and needed.

Suddenly, out of the corner of my eye I caught sight of a beautiful butterfly, resting on a flowered branch nearby. I felt great joy and the deepest gratitude.

There were no scissors in sight.

Acknowledgments

First, I want to acknowledge my dear friend, Jody Pike, who has been with me on this writing journey from the beginning. Her enthusiasm and support have kept me going. Thanks to my new writing friends at Regents Point, Vivian Johnson, and Shirley Mitchell, for their observations and encouragement. And my thanks and deep gratitude to my close friends and colleagues, Lynne Haigh and Glenda Walther, who have been so present and supportive over the years. To Thelma Jean Goodrich, a great listener, who has been an actual witness to some of the stories. To my editor, Brooke Warner, for her clarity, wisdom, and expertise. To my children and stepchildren, who have brought about such joy into my life, and who keep me learning. And finally, to my beloved husband, Bob Hilton, who truly is the "pearl of great price."

About the Author

Virginia Wink Hilton, PhD, is a retired psychotherapist, who has published numerous articles for colleagues in her field. Her first memoir, *Memories: Many Roads to Home: The First Phase: The Texas Years,* about growing up in Texas, was published in 2014. She lives in Irvine, California, with her husband, Robert Hilton.

www.ingramcontent.com/pod-product-compliance
Lightning Source LLC
Chambersburg PA
CBHW020904080526
44589CB00011B/442